Beyond Cut, Copy and Paste

Beyond Cut, Copy and Paste

Dig deeper into the world of Microsoft Word, Excel and PowerPoint

Henry Balogun Ph.D.

iUniverse, Inc.
New York Lincoln Shanghai

Beyond Cut, Copy and Paste
Dig deeper into the world of Microsoft Word, Excel and PowerPoint

iUniverse, Inc.
an imprint of iUniverse, Inc.

For information address:
iUniverse
2021 Pine Lake Road, Suite 100
Lincoln, NE 68512
www.iuniverse.com

ISBN: 0-595-27339-4

Printed in the United States of America

DEDICATION

To Mari Fukushima

It was one of those rare Monday mornings anyone would have loved to keep on auto play for a long time. I woke up saying to myself (in reference to the week before); "Wow, that was one tough week! Everything that could have gone wrong went wrong." So, I looked at my girlfriend, Mari Fukushima, and said to her: "I'm going to write a book." I was expecting some sarcastic response but to my surprise, she turned around and asked gently "about what?"

"I'm going to write about how to get more from your computer applications such as Microsoft Office and then (if possible) write about programming. My goal is to simplify them in such a way that it would increase the current number of computer users all around the world." I thought she was going to give me the American interpretation of what I just told her. Again, she acted contrary to my expectations when she said affirmatively: "I think you should and I am very serious. You are a very intelligent and a consummate professional who takes his work seriously. As a psychotherapist, your patients love you to death—most especially when they see changes in their lives within a short period of time. And when you try to explain things, you break it down to a level anyone with a half brain should be able to understand. You are very good and I seriously think you should write the book."

I looked around to see if I was talking to an impostor but it was her with a beaming smile on her face. I wanted to ask, "Did anyone pay you to say this stuff you just said about me?" Instead, I was so surprised and shocked at such a positive evaluation of me, and I said to her; "If I ever wrote the book, I'm going to dedicate it to you."

Here it is and it's all because of you and your believing in me. Thank you babe!

ACKNOWLEDGMENT

First and foremost, I thank God for giving me the spirit of a sound mind. It has always been my desire to always look for easier way to explain what seem like a complex and difficult to understand subject such as computer application and programming. This book, I believe, is the first step in making that desire a reality.

I thank those whose words and deeds helped me to see clearly. I am sincerely grateful to those who took time out of their busy schedules to carefully scrutinize every page in this book and made useful suggestions. My sincere thanks to Caroline Mary Singleton, John Ogunkorode and Crystal Morrison who went over each step to be sure that no stone was left unturned.

I thank my children: Sam, Eunice, Joshua and Maryann. You guys are precious than silver and gold. Without you, life is meaningless. Thanks for your daily inspiration, cooperation and love.

Finally, thanks to those who genuinely remembered me in their prayers. "Your labor is not in vain in the Lord."

INTRODUCTION

Another difficult computer book, huh? No. *Beyond Cut, Copy and Paste* is not just a computer book. It is all about providing computer solutions. This is a book for you regardless of your computer background, knowledge and experience. This is not about terabyte, gigabyte, or binary code—you know, the techno-stuff that can send an average person looking for Tylenol for migraine! I don't do stuff like that. You can ask all my friends and they'll tell you I'm the nicest guy in the universe. I'm telling you this is a simple book designed to help you master your *Microsoft Word 2000* as well as your *Word XP* effortlessly. It is a book for everyone—expert and novice.

My primary goal is to provide a high quality, innovative, fun and solutions oriented management tool. My writing philosophy is that the first and the last tasks of a writer and educator are to keep interest alive. This book depicts a real life work environment, thereby making it easier to understand the delicate and technologically packed world of *Word, Graphic and Data* processing. This is the first of a series geared toward providing solutions. You don't have to be a computer genius to use this book. And anyone desiring to understand the sophisticated world of computer technology should not be labeled "dummy." So, this is not a book for dummy, it is for you the inquiry minds of the world. It is full of graphical interface designed to guide you along the way.

"Not too long ago computers were large, impersonal machines hidden away in glass-enclosed, climate-controlled rooms. To use one, you had to either prepare a deck of punched cards and hand them to a professional operator or type cryptic commands, line by line, on a terminal. Today, computers are as accessible and personal as you want them to be." They are less intimidating and continuously opening the door of opportunities to those desiring to understand, in order to become a computer expert, or better yet, Information Technology (IT) professionals.

Within the last decade, word processing software has evolved into a sophisticated, programming oriented and indispensable business tool that can be used by businesses of all sizes. This is a phenomenon that I personally have experienced not only as a student but as a first hand business participant at virtually all levels. If you have not been using a computer, the time to begin is now.

Many people would like to know everything there is to know about the combination of *Word, Graphic and Data* processing now known as Microsoft Office programs but they are too intimidated by overwhelming abbreviations and terminologies. To make this dream a reality for all the daring souls willing to burn the midnight oil in the interest of learning, I've decided to offer a simple but knowledge packed approach, designed to meet the need for varying skill levels. This is the beginning of a new series. Every step and function presented in this book has been tested and proven in most of the Instructor-led classroom training I've offered, geared toward certification in *Microsoft Office User Specialist (MOUS) Program*. Now you can use them in your daily activities. Each section is focused and complete.

Who should use this book?

If you are concerned about what is under the hood of *Microsoft Office* as well as how to use and customize the programs *in Microsoft Office*, this book is for you. If you want to do most of what you thought only the experts can do, this book is for you. If you are concerned about improving your skills, or acquiring a new skill, this book is for you. If you are looking for a book written with the intent to teach you everything you need to become one of the elites in the field of Information Technology without wrapping you in techno jargons and unnecessary terminologies, then, this book is for you. If you are looking for a book that is easy to understand using real life examples, you are looking at it. Hey, when you become an expert, don't forget to send me a thank you note. My little girl, Maryann, will really appreciate that. Don't tell her I asked you to send it!

Fine-tuning Your Computer System

Optional Configuration

Beyond Cut, Copy and Paste is designed to bring you into the beautiful world of automation, integration and animation while addressing functions of management. But before we begin, we are going to make some minor adjustment (remember, this is optional) to simplify movement within the system.

First of all, you may want to change the icons on your desktop from using double click to a single click everywhere. If that is the case, let's perform these simple steps together.

Steps

1. Click **Start** and then move your mouse to **Programs** from the list of programs in your system, look for and click on **Windows Explorer**. (If you are using Windows XP, click the **Start** button, put the mouse on **All Programs** and then click **My Computer**.)
2. Click **Tools** → **Folder Options**. (for those using Windows 98, ME and 2000, click **Settings**). That should take you to a screen that looks like the following:

3. Click the **General** tab, in the **Click items as follows** section, click on the radio button labeled **Single-click to open an item (point to select)**

4. Click **Ok.**

From now on, all you will need to access any icon (on your desktop and virtually everywhere) is a single-click and not double-click anymore.2

Do you know that you can change the new *Windows XP* start menu? If you don't like the default start menu, you can change it to the *Classic Start* menu you are used to, thereby making it look like your *Windows 95, 98, ME* and even *2000* start menu.

To change your Start menu:

1. **Right Click** on the **Start** button _____ or anywhere on the **Taskbar**

2. Click **Properties**

3. When the *Taskbar and Start Menu Properties* window pops up, click the **Start Menu** tab and then click the radio button next to **Classic Start menu**

4. Click **Ok**

Work from the same window

If you are like me, a nice guy who prefers to have any new item in my computer open in the same window, you are going to like this one. As for me, I get frustrated with the clutter created by a new window opening separately, most especially, when I'm using Windows Explorer. Yeah, what about my desk! Don't even go there. I like it the way it is. I'm talking about cluttering up your computer screen with so many windows. Do you know you can solve this problem easily! Let me show you how

Windows 98

1. In My Computer or Windows Explorer, Choose **View → Folder Options.**
2. Click to activate the **General** tab (if not already activated) on the *Folder Options* window
3. Click the radio button next to **Custom, based on settings you choose,** and then click **Settings**
4. From the *Custom Settings* window, click **Open each folder in the same window.**
5. Click **Ok.**

Windows XP

1. In My Computer, choose **Tools → Folder Options.**
2. Click to activate the **General** tab (if not already activated) on the *Folder Options* window.
3. Click the radio button next to **Open each folder in the same window.**
4. Click **Ok.**

Add a little more speed to your system

Windows 98

1. Click **Start → Programs → Accessories** and from the **System Tools,** click **Disk Defragmenter.** This should take you to a small pop up window.
2. Click **Settings** and on the Disk Defragmenter Settings, click to place a check mark in the check box next to **Rearrange program files so my programs start faster.**
3. Click **Ok.**

Windows XP

1. Click **Start** → **All Programs** → **Accessories** and from the **System Tools,** click **Disk Defragmenter.** This should take you to a small pop up window.

2. On the Disk Defragmenter window, click one of the following:

   a. Analyze

   b. Defragment

3. When you have finished, simply close the window

Notepad

Whenever you see this arrow → always remember that when you perform the action preceding it, the next is the action to which the arrow is pointing. I like to do this to avoid writing long sentences. Isn't that cool! Wait a minute; did you just call me lazy? I'm going to get you for this—no doubt.

This book assumes you are no stranger to Windows Applications. It also assumes you are well skilled in typing. Although this is not a book about typing, using Word Processing involves typing most of the time. Try as much as possible to improve your typing skills.

Notepad

Do not rush through the steps in this book. If you mistakenly click a choice different from what is suggested, don't panic. Take time to read whatever pops up and gracefully get out of it before you do anything else. Not only that, always make sure to finish each step before moving to the next. You are not trying to run faster than the man in front. In this case, you are the man in front. Don't try to outrun yourself. Just follow each step carefully. Good luck!

CONTENTS

Chapter One

What is Microsoft Office?

Microsoft Office is a family of computer programs bundles up into one. They call it (Microsoft) Office not because it is meant for use in an office environment only even though most of the programs in Microsoft Office are geared toward office users. However, Microsoft Office (comprised of *Word, Excel, PowerPoint, Outlook, Access* and in most cases *FrontPage*) is for you regardless of what you intend to use it for—personal use or business use. *Beyond Cut, Copy and Paste* is designed to help you in your quest to fully understand these three programs:

1. *Microsoft Word.* This is a program designed to "assist you in virtually every aspect of document creation." If you are a constant user of word processing software, get on the band wagon of the most widely used word processing program on the planet.

2. *Microsoft Excel.* This is a program popularly known as an electronic spreadsheet designed to make working with numbers (regardless of whether you are actually comfortable working with numbers or not) something to really enjoy and not something to despise. There is simply no better electronic spreadsheet or worksheet as some people like to refer to it.

3. *PowerPoint.* There is no program capable of enabling any professional to create multimedia presentation like *PowerPoint.* However, one thing *PowerPoint* doesn't do contrary to public opinion is create presentation—people do. PowerPoint is a tool. You can use this powerful program to create visual aids necessary to give an exquisite presentation. I am going to show you how you can create stunning PowerPoint slides, pictures, sounds, video clips, music, animations, charts and a host of other elements.

These programs graphical user interface makes them so easy even a first time user will start doing meaningful things right from day one. What about their integration with the rest of Office programs as well as web integration! Just what the doctor ordered. Their powerful charting and formatting features make displaying your data (any way you so desire) something to talk about. Go ahead and turn on your computer system and let us explore the wonderful world of *Microsoft Word, Excel and PowerPoint.* Oh, one more thing, we are going beyond just cut, copy and paste. In that wise, I expect you to have at a minimum knowledge of how to use the mouse—that's all the preliminary knowledge you are expected to have. Is that too much to expect? If you don't, I strongly advise you take "Mouse Click 101" don't ask me who is offering it and where, I have no idea.

To Start Word

- From the desktop, click on **Start** button usually located at the bottom left corner of your desktop.

- Place your mouse on **Programs,** or **All Programs** (if your system is equipped with Windows XP) from the right pane, look for and select **Microsoft Word.**

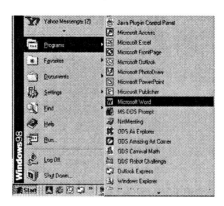

- Microsoft Word will open and the title bar will say "Microsoft Word—Document 1" In case a "Tip of the Day" appears on your screen when you open Word, you must click on **Ok** after reading it, to close the dialog window.

If you already have your **Microsoft Office shortcut bar** loaded on your desktop, click 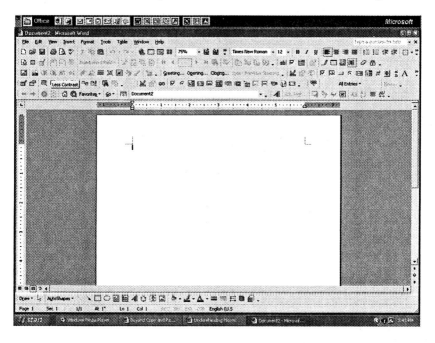 button on the **shortcut bar** to open **Word**. Opening your Microsoft Word should take you to a screen similar to the following:

If your screen doesn't look exactly like mine, don't worry. I usually have a lot of toolbars open for quick and easy access. I'm not trying to show off my beautiful screen shot, am I? I just want to let you know that here is where you do all your creating, editing, formatting, automation, integration and animation of document(s).

The Access Keys

Let us look carefully at the menu choices available in your Microsoft Word and you will discover that some letters are underlined and some are not.

<u>F</u>ile <u>E</u>dit <u>V</u>iew <u>I</u>nsert F<u>o</u>rmat <u>T</u>ools T<u>a</u>ble <u>W</u>indow <u>H</u>elp

The underlined letters are called **Access Keys**. Let's assume that something happened and you are freaking out because you think Freddie Kruger is in the room, and let's also assume that in the process of trying to kill Freddie you mistakenly step over your mouse and break it into little pieces, don't worry about the mouse. All you need to do is hold down the **Alt** key and press F. This will take you to where you can E<u>x</u>it gracefully—no, not from the room but from your Microsoft Word. After that, you can easily turn around and deal with Freddie in your own way.

Each underlined letter works with the **Alt** key. Hold down the **Alt** key and then press any of the **Access Keys** (the underlined letter) and it will activate the pull down menu. On the pull down menu, you will discover that some letters are also underlined; you can just press any of those without using the **Alt** key. For example: to open a file without using the mouse

1. Hold down the **Alt** key and press **F**
2. On the pull down menu, press **O** and that will activate the **Open** dialog window.
3. From the **Open** dialog window you will have to use the **Alt** key again along with any of the **Access Keys** showing in your **Open** dialog window to access the area of interest to you.

This does not mean that you should just go ahead and get rid of your mouse, ok? We all like the point and click, don't we?

Minor Configurations in Word

For the sake of the project we are about to do together, we are going to make some minor adjustment to your system. The first will involve making sure the system knows your name, initial and address so we would not have to input them every time we need them. The second will be to inform the system about some common abbreviations we are going to be using. After that, we are going to require every toolbar button to display shortcuts as well. The last minor configuration necessary for our project will have to do with the way Microsoft Office display menu options once we click on it or activate it using any of the access keys.

Let's go ahead and put your name, initial and address in the system if you don't already have them there.

Steps

1. On **Tools,** click **Options** and you should see a screen exactly like the following:

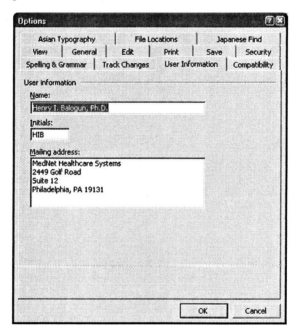

2. Click the **User Information** tab to enter your <u>Name,</u> followed by <u>Initials</u> and <u>Mailing Address.</u>

The next one is **AutoCorrect.**
One of many features of *Microsoft office* you are really going to appreciate is AutoCorrect. With AutoCorrect you can type a word or abbreviation and Word will replace it with the exact text you specified in the AutoCorrect dialog window. This is a feature perfect for legal, medical, or other specialized

environment. Type an abbreviation, and AutoCorrect will convert it to the correct word or phrase.

When you type a word already specified in the list incorrectly, it will automatically be corrected. By default, the AutoCorrect feature already includes many commonly misspelled words. Needless to say, you can go ahead and add your own problem words to the AutoCorrect list. That is exactly what we are going to do right now.

Steps

1. To create a new AutoCorrect entry, choose **Tools** → **AutoCorrect**.

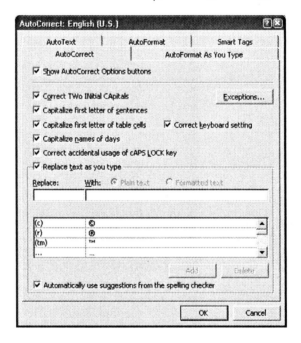

2. Type the misspelled word or abbreviation in the **Replace text box**. For the sake of our project here let us type ADHD.

3. Type the correct word or phrase in the **With text box**. Let's type Attention Deficit Hyperactivity Disorder,

4. Click the **Add** button to add more to the list. Add the following primary diagnosis:

Replace	With
ODD	Oppositional Defiant Disorder
PDD	Pervasive Developmental Disorder
DBD	Disruptive Behavior Disorder NOS
AISD	Alcohol-Induced Sleep Disorder
OCD	Obsessive Compulsive Disorder
PTSD	Posttraumatic Stress Disorder

5. Click **OK** when you are finished adding entries.

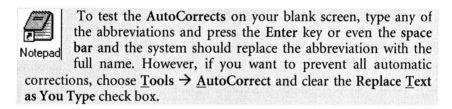

To test the **AutoCorrects** on your blank screen, type any of the abbreviations and press the **Enter** key or even the space bar and the system should replace the abbreviation with the full name. However, if you want to prevent all automatic corrections, choose **Tools → AutoCorrect** and clear the **Replace Text as You Type** check box.

Show Shortcut Keys in ScreenTips

What is Screen Tips? To put it simply, screen tips tells you what an icon or a button is all about and if anything, what it is supposed to do. Move your mouse over to any of the toolbar buttons now displayed on your screen and you will see either a name or description of the button. To help you master some of the shortcuts available in your Microsoft Office, we are going to configure those buttons to show shortcut keys along with the name or description of each button. Please bear in mind that this feature works perfectly fine in all of Microsoft Office applications except Excel. To display shortcut keys in ScreenTips:

Steps

1. On the **Tools** menu, click **Customize**, and then click the **Options** tab.

2. If it's not already selected, select the **Show ScreenTips on toolbars** check box.

3. Select the **Show shortcut keys in ScreenTips** check box.

Show All Menu Commands in Office 2000

Microsoft Office 2000 and *Office XP* are both designed to display only the commands that you use most often each time you click any of the menu option. However, if you want to see all of the commands at once like in Office 97, which is not impossible. To avoid confusion and statement such as: "I can't find the choice the book is asking me to click," we are going to ask the system to display menu choices on click. To turn off personalized menus:

1. On the **Tools** menu, click **Customize**, and then click the **Options** tab.
2. To show all the commands on the menus, clear the **Menus show recently used commands first** check box. (In Microsoft Office XP, you will click the check box that says **Always show full menus.**)

Can you believe that once you've done it in one of *Microsoft Office 2000 or XP* program you've done it in all! Yep, I'm telling you, you are becoming a force to reckon with. There are some other configurations we could have made but for now we are just going to move right along into the real reason the book is written.

CHAPTER TWO

Business Letter and mass mailing

Let me introduce you to Ms. Jones. She is the Clinical Director of MidMed, a very large Outpatient Psychiatry right here in this beloved city of ours. Not long ago, she requested to have a separate Microsoft Office 2000 installed in her Secretary's computer system. This is in addition to having access to the one already installed in the company's Network Server. Our job is to assist Ms. Jones' Secretary to get more done in less time. She is going to be overwhelmed unless we lend a helping hand. Notwithstanding, the time to get more organized in order to become much more effective and efficient is now.

Ms. Jones would like to find a way to automate her clinic functions. She is under pressure from management to cut cost and increase productivity. Her first strategy is to create documentation on demand. According to her, this would lead to elimination of wasteful spending. She is meeting with the Medical Director as well as other staff members next week to discuss centralization of Intake, Scheduling, Medical Record and Assignment of Patient per Clinician.

The first assignment is to find a way to eliminate patient no-shows, thereby reducing idle time on the part of both Psychiatrists (Clinicians) and Therapists. To accomplish this productivity driven objective, we are going to help her Secretary to develop a letter that she can use to remind every patient (on demand) not to forget about previously scheduled appointments with Psychiatrists and Therapists in the clinic. We are determined to help her Secretary develop whatever other documentations are required. We've got to do a good job because Ms. Jones is a consummate professional who will not settle for anything less than the best.

Assumptions

- We are going to assume that the clinic does not have a standard letter-head for this type of correspondence. In that wise, we are going to create one right now for the letter we are about to develop for the clinic.

- We are also going to assume that there is no existing data source (data-base) to pull from and in that case, we are going to create a data source to accommodate all the 1500 patients of the clinic. What? C'mon, this is really nothing to sneeze about. The front desk clerk is very good and gen-uinely believes in team work. She is going to help us input information into our data source as soon as it is created. In this case, your job is just to create and the front desk people will do the rest. Is that fair enough?

Creating Personalized Letterhead

To create a professionally looking letter head, let us follow this simple step-by-step approach. It is not advisable to skip any of the steps or assume you know it before attempting it. Let us do it together.

Steps

1. Choose **File → Page Setup**. Set the top margin to 0.5"

2. Click **Ok**

3. Click **Format → Font** and that should give you a screen like the following:

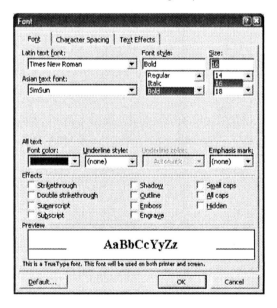

4. Under **Font style,** choose **Bold.** Under **Size,** choose **16** and under **Font color,** choose **Dark Red.**

5. Click **Ok.**

6. Type **MidMed** and press **Enter.**

7. Click **Align Right** or simply use the shortcut which is **Ctrl + R**

8. Repeat step 3 above but don't forget to change the **Size** to **11** and under **Font color,** choose **Dark Blue.**

9. Click **Ok.**

10. Type the following exactly as written below—single spaced.

2359 Lakewood Road,
Philadelphia, PA 19142
Phone (215) 555-1212
Fax (215) 555-6767

11. Click **Align Left** or **Ctrl + L** to move the cursor (not the address you just typed) back to the left.

When you finish, your screen should look similar to the following:

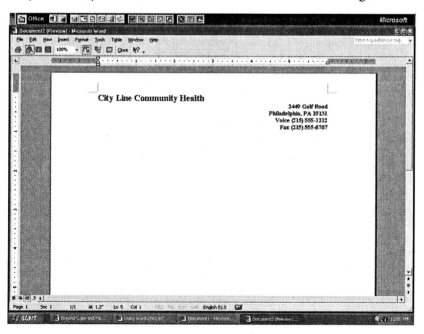

Let us save this portion as a template. In that wise, we can always come back to use it again and again. But before we do, Let us not forget that this is a project and the letterhead we just created is the first among many documents including data source (database) we are going to create for this project. One thing we would like to do is keep our project well organized.

Organizing a project

Our number one goal is to create a project folder (directory). This would make it easier for us to locate any file created as part of this project. I am going to urge you not to rush but follow these steps very carefully.

12. Click the **Save** button or simply go to **File → Save** and the following screen pops up.

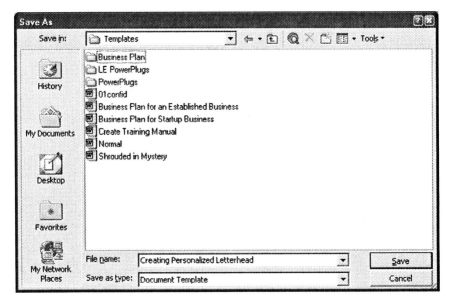

13. Click the arrow next to the **Save in** box and select **Local Disk (C:)**. What this means is that your new directory is going to be placed in the root directory of your C Drive.

14. After that, move your mouse (don't click) on the second manila folder to the right of the **Save in** box and it should read **Create New Folder.** Click on it and you should see the following screen:

15. In the <u>N</u>ame box, type **"Practice Folder"** as the name of your new directory or folder.

16. Click **Ok.**

17. Type a name for your letter head in the **File <u>n</u>ame** box

18. In **Save as <u>T</u>ype,** click **the arrow** next to the box and choose **Document Template.**

19. It is very likely that the name showing in the **Save in** box has changed to "Template." Kindly make sure you are paying close attention. If that is the case, click on the box itself, choose **Local Disk (C:)** and you should see a directory named "Practice Folder" (the directory you created in steps 12 through to 16). Click the directory, and then

20. Click **Save.**

Exiting Word

After using Word or any of the programs or applications in Microsoft Office (or any other program for that matter), you should always make the effort to exit the application gracefully. Microsoft Word is designed to perform necessary housekeeping before it closes.

If after you click save you decided to modify your document and let's assume that changes to the document have not been saved, any attempt to exit will compel Word to bring out a small pop up window asking the following question:

Do you want to save the changes to "File Name"

All you need to do is click **Yes** for Word to save changes to your document before leaving the program.

Saving All Your Files at Once

In case you have more than one document open in Word, you can save them all at once or close them all at once. Anything that can help improve productivity is excellent in a busy office environment. Let us unfold some of the hidden secrets and helpful hints of Microsoft Word.

1. Hold down the **Shift** key and click **File** menu. When you hold down **Shift**, two new options appear on the **File** menu that wouldn't appear ordinarily: **Close All** and **Save All**.

2. If you have more than one document open and you want to save them all, click **Save All**.

3. To close all your open documents, click **Close All**; In this case, Word will prompt you to save your changes before closing any documents.

To exit *Word* gracefully, choose **File** followed by **Exit**. For the sake of our project, let us exit *Word* right now.

Opening an Existing Document

There are several ways you can open an existing document. One way is to go straight from your desktop to the document you were working on last. Your Windows operating system is designed to remember some of your most recent files making it easier to open any of those files. Another way is to open Word and then open any of your existing documents. Let us try opening our last document from the desktop.

From Windows XP

Click **Start** and place your mouse on **My Recent Documents**. There you will see the list of your most recent documents. Click on the one you want to open and that should activate and open *Microsoft Word* along with the document.

From Windows 95, 98, ME and 2000

Click **Start** and place your mouse on **Documents**. There you will see the list of your most recent documents. Click on the one you want to open and that should activate and open *Microsoft Word* along with the document.

From inside Word

1. Choose **File → Open** or click the **Open** button on the Standard toolbar, or simply hold down the **Ctrl** key and press **O**. Either way should take you to the following window:

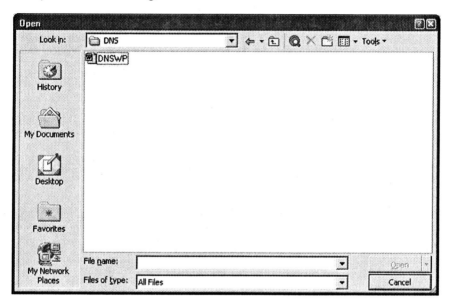

2. Click on the **Look In** box to select the drive followed by the folder where the document you want to open is located and the contents of the folder should appear. In our case, let us open our last document—the Letter Head Template.

3. Once the file is located, click on it once and click **Open**.

Open more than one file at once

4. To open more than one file at the same time, click **on the first file**, hold down the **Ctrl** key while you click **on the second file** and **the third** and... Once all the files you want to open are highlighted, click **Open**.

Before going to the next chapter, kindly make sure the letterhead you created earlier is now open and active on your screen.

CHAPTER THREE

Working with Document

We are going to type the following letter exactly as it is into the template we have created, saved and now opened. We are going to use single space within paragraph and double space between paragraphs. We are going to type it with all the mistakes, extra spaces in paragraph one, and with all the spelling errors just exactly as they are (please do not make corrections while you are typing). As for the special characters such as © and ½ do not worry about trying to insert those right now. You will have the chance to insert them later on.

In a standard business letter, information is typically left-justified (along the left margin) and flows down the page in the following order:

1. Current date
2. Recipient's name and address
3. Salutation (opening greeting)
4. Body of the letter, containing the text or message of the letter
5. Complimentary closing followed by a comma. Example of acceptable complimentary closing is "Sincerely"
6. Signature block (name on one line followed by the title on the next line). There are usually four spaces between "Sincerely" and the signature block
7. Reference initial—this usually contains the initial of the typist in lowercase
8. Enclosure notification follows
9. Copy notation is usually the last line. Example: c: Henry I. Balogun, Ph.D.

MidMed©

2449 Golf Road
Philadelphia, PA 19131
Voice (215) 555-1212
Fax (215) 555-6767

March 24, 2003

Dear

This is to remind you of your previously schduled appointment with for Medication check on Thursday, January 29, 2003 at 10:30 am, and also with for psychotherapy at 11:00 am. You are hereby adviced to arrive early. Your total time at the clinic is expected to be 1½ hours.

If you have any questions or concerns, or you are going to be late for whatever reasons, feel free to call me at (215) 999-6161 or call your Psychiatrist and Therapist directly. Their numbers are as following:

When coming, kindly remember to bring the follown with you:

Insurance card
Social Security card; and
Photo identification

Sincerely,

Maria Villanueva
Secretary

cm
Enclosure
c: Front Desk Personnel

Create Database Using Mail Merge

There is currently no data source that contains the list of names and addresses for the patients at the clinic where Ms. Jones works. We are going to create one using the *Mail Merge Helper*. This is not the only way we can create the data source. You can also use address information from *Outlook and Schedule+*. Not only that, there are some third party applications such as Medical Billing or Practice Management software that will let you integrate with its database using

Microsoft Word or Excel. Regardless of how your data source (database) is created, we need to create the main document first and that is what you did earlier.

A main document could be a letter, an envelope, agreement or other document that you would like to send to a lot of people or perhaps one person at a time through the convenience of mail merge. They usually contain codes that will be replaced with entries from a data source of names and addresses. The main document has the Mail Merge Helper button on the Mail Merge toolbar, which is the launching point for the other Mail Merge tasks. When creating a main document for a mail merge, you can use an existing document or create a new document. In either case, you need to define the document as the main document for the mail merge. In our case, we are going to use the document we created earlier.

Notepad

The Mail Merge helper interface shown here is taken from Microsoft Office 2000. If you are using Microsoft Office XP, please visit www.mednetservices.com to download instructions on how to use mail merge in Office XP.

Steps

1. Open the existing document.

2. Choose <u>Tools</u> → **Mail Merge** to display the Mail Merge Helper. The next screen is going to look exactly like this:

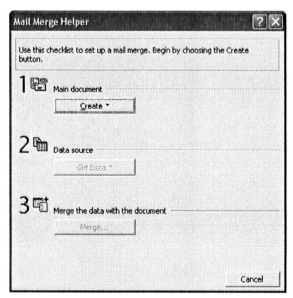

3. Click the <u>C</u>reate button under Step 1 Main document, and then select Form <u>L</u>etters.

4. Word will give you a choice to use the <u>A</u>ctive Window, which is the document window that is open behind the dialog window. Or, start a <u>N</u>ew Main Document, which will open a new blank document window. In this case, we are going to click the Active Window.

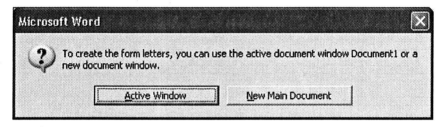

5. Word takes you back to the Mail Merge Helper dialog window, which now displays the type of merge and the name and *path* of the document under the Main Document step.

6. You are now ready to choose <u>G</u>et Data under Step 2 Data Source, or <u>E</u>dit the Main Document under Step 1.

7. Choose <u>G</u>et Data under Step 2 on the dialog window; then choose <u>C</u>reate Data Source to display the following Create Data Source dialog window.

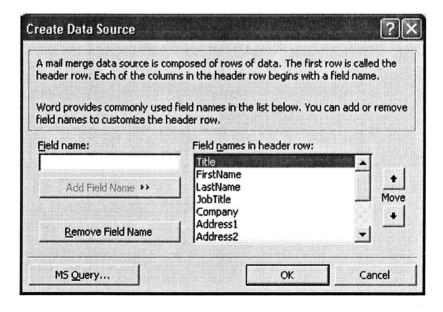

8. Scroll through the list of fields in the **Field Names in Header Row** list box to see commonly used field names provided by Word.

   a. If you see any field names you won't use in your main document, select the name from the list, and then choose the **Remove Field Name button**. In this case, let us select "Country" from the list and then click **Remove Field Name**. After that, feel free to remove "Title," "Job Title," "Company," and "WorkPhone."

   b. To add a field name that isn't listed, type the name in the **Field Name** text box, then choose **Add Field Name**. For the sake of our project, we are going to add the following field names (Word 2000 will not accept space. This is regarded as an invalid character):

Prefix	Clinician	Therapist
PrimDiagnosis	SecDiagnosis	AdmDate
DateOfBirth	SSNumber	PrimCarePhy
ClinAvailability	ClinPhoneNumber	TherpAvailability
TherpPhoneNumber		

   Don't forget to delete the following field names as mentioned earlier:

Title	JobTitle	Company
Country	WorkPhone	FaxPhone

   c. To change the sequence of field names, select a field name in the **Field Names** in **Header Row** list box, then click the extreme right up-arrow or down-arrow buttons. The top-to-bottom order of the fields is the order the fields will appear for data entry in the data source.

9. Edit the list of field names and when finished, choose **OK**.

10. Word displays the following **Save As** dialog window. In the **File Name** box, enter a name such as (Patient Database) for the data source document and choose **Save**.

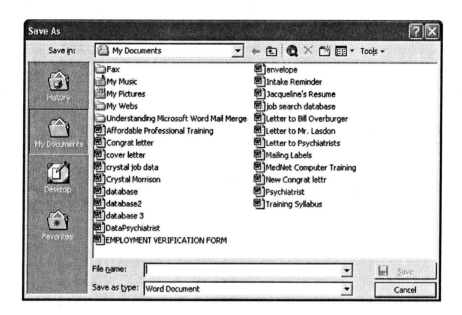

11. The next screen is a decision box; choose **Edit Data Source** to enter information into the data source file you just created, or choose **Edit Main Document** to insert *merge fields* into the main document. But for now, we are going to choose **Edit Data Source**.

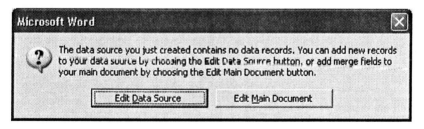

We are going to input the following into our database. Don't forget to use the tab key to go to the next field and once you finish the first set of patient record, click **Add New** to key in the rest.

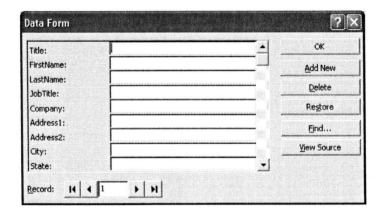

Data to input (always use the tab key to go to the next field and when you finish, click **Add New** to add more data and when you finish inputting all patient record, click **Ok**).

Prefix:	Ms	Ms	Mr	Mr.
FirstName:	Jane	Maria	Ryan	Jose
LastName:	Dickson	Ramos	Roberts	Santiago
Address1:	2941 Map Rd.	671 Long Island Ave	2449 Street Road	9572 New Haven Road
Address2:	D – 2851	5421	B – 231	C – 951
City:	Motown	Middletown	Philadelphia	Bensalem
State:	PA	PA	PA	PA
PostalCode:	02901	01913	19031	01921
HomePhone:	(215) 555-1212	(215) 555-6565	(215) 555-7979	(215) 555-8989
DateOfBirth:	03/04/1989	11/27/1988	04/30/1990	07/21/1988
SSNumber:	021-44-6789	212-31-5423	212-45-2178	022-41-8922
AdmDate:	12/02/2002	12/04/2002	12/02/2002	01/23/2003
Clinician:	H. Desmond, MD	E. Dada, MD	E. Balogun, MD	L. Ginger, MD
ClinAvailabiligy:	M – F (9:00 – 4:00)	M – F (9:00 – 4:00)	M – F (9:00 – 4:00)	M – F (9:00 – 4:00)
ClinPhoneNumber:	215-777-9191	215-777-9192	215-777-9193	215-777-9194
Therapist:	M. Sukukowa	Liz Catherine	Mike Luther	M. Fukushima
TherpAvailability:	M - F (9:00 – 7:00)	M - F (9:00 – 7:00)	M - F (9:00 – 7:00)	M - F (9:00 – 7:00)
TherpPhoneNumber:	215-777-8282	215-777-8283	215-777-8284	215-777-8285
PrimDiagnosis:	OCD	ADHD	ADHD	PTSD
SecDiagnosis:	None	ODD	ODD	Depressive Disorder NOS
PrimCarePhy:	D'Angelo, MD	L. Dada, MD	J. Santiago, MD	N. Gubloan

Inserting Merge Fields to your Document

Once you have completed the establishment of a *data source* for your mail merge, you are ready to insert *merge fields* in the main document. Merge fields are the variable information that changes for each document. The document could be a letter, envelope, labels, form, invoice, or agreement, or any document such as a newsletter or even a brochure. In addition to your existing toolbar, you will see two new buttons. One is labeled **Insert Merge Field** and the other one is labeled **Insert Word Field**

Steps

1. I'm quite sure the main document is still open, right? However, if the main document is not open with the Mail Merge toolbar displayed, click the Mail Merge Helper button on the toolbar. Click <u>E</u>dit under Step 1 Main Document, and then select the main document from the displayed list.

2. Position the insertion point where you want a merge field to appear. In this case, position your cursor (the insertion point) two spaces below the date. Click the **Insert Merge Field** button on the Mail Merge toolbar, and then select the field from the list presented.

3. In our case, we are going to start inserting the following field names exactly as they are written below:

   > March 26, 2003
   >
   > «Prefix» «First_Name» «Last_Name»
   > «Address_Line_1»
   > «Address_Line_2»
   > «City», «State» «ZIP_Code»
   >
   > Dear «Prefix» «Last_Name»

4. In the first paragraph, insert the field name for both the **Clinician** and the **Therapist** exactly as you see it in the following document. When you finish, your main document should look exactly like the one below.

MidMed©

2449 Golf Road
Philadelphia, PA 19131
Voice (215) 555-1212
Fax (215) 555-6767

January 23, 2003

«Prefix» «First_Name» «Last_Name»
«Address_Line_1»
«Address_Line_2»
«City», «State» «ZIP_Code»

Dear «Prefix» «Last_Name»:

This is to remind you of your previously schduled appointment with «Clinician» for Medication check on Thursday, January 29, 2003 at 10:30 am, and also with «Therapist» for psychotherapy at 11:00 am. You are hereby adviced to arrive early. Your total time at the clinic is expected to be 1½ hours.

If you have any questions or concerns, or you are going to be late for whatever reasons, feel free to call me at (215) 999-6161 or call your Psychiatrist and Therapist directly. Their numbers are as following:

When coming, kindly remember to bring the followng with you:

Insurance card
Social Security card; and
Photo identification

Sincerely,

Maria Villanueva
Secretary

cm
Enclosure
c: Front Desk Personnel

CHAPTER FOUR

Document Editing and Formatting

The time to correct our mistakes, and produce an error free document has come. In Microsoft Office, you can copy or cut information from within a document and paste it at a different location in the same document. You can also do the same thing between documents, or even between two different applications in Microsoft Office or any application compatible with any of the Microsoft Office applications.

Before we do anything with our project, there is some really neat stuff I want you to fully understand regarding document editing and formatting. To handle the tasks before us quickly and professionally, we are going to go over some basics. These include highlighting, deleting and replacing, copy or cut and paste includes undo, redo and more.

Let us begin by learning "selecting" or "highlighting" text. Kindly bear in mind that when you see "selecting" mentioned, I am basically referring to "highlighting." In this case, both "selecting" and "highlighting" will be referred to interchangeably.

How to highlight text

Steps

1. Press and hold down the **left** mouse button. Move the mouse pointer to the other end of the text. Release the mouse button only when the text you want to select is highlighted.
2. Place the cursor at the beginning of the text you want to highlight. Press and hold down the **Shift** key with one finger while holding down the

right arrow key with another finger. Release both when the text you want to select is highlighted.

3. If the cursor is blinking at the end of the word you want to highlight, press and hold down the **Shift** key with one finger while holding down the **left arrow** key with another finger. Release both when the text you want to select is highlighted.

4. To select a word, place the mouse (the "I" beam) anywhere on the word to be highlighted. Double click the left mouse button. The word you selected is now highlighted.

5. To select or highlight an entire line of text, place the cursor at the begin-ning of the line you want to highlight, press and hold down the **Shift** key and press the **End** key once, or place the cursor at the end of the line you want to highlight, press and hold down the **Shift** key and press the **Home** key once.

6. To select or highlight an entire document, choose **Edit → Select All**, or hold down the **Ctrl** key and press **A** once.

7. To remove highlight without deleting the highlighted text, <u>Do not</u> press any key on the keyboard other than the arrow key—whichever one.

Cut and Paste.

Steps

1. Select (highlight) the information you want to move. In this case, we are going to highlight all of the second paragraph

2. Press **Ctrl + X** or click the **Cut** button on the Standard toolbar, or simply choose **Edit → Cut**.

3. Move the insertion point (the cursor) to two spaces below "Photo iden-tification."

4. Press **Ctrl + V** or click the **Paste** button on the Standard toolbar or choose **Edit → Paste**

Notepad

To quickly move text or graphics to another location in the same document, select the information you want to move. Move the mouse pointer onto the selected area and drag the selection to the new or desired location. This feature is called drag and drop.

Delete

1. Place the cursor at the beginning of the word you want to erase

2. Press the **delete key** to erase the first letter

3. **Continue to press the delete key** until everything you want to erase is gone.

Backspace

1. Place the cursor at the end of the word you want to erase

2. Press the **backspace** key and it will back over the letter and erase it

3. **Continue to press the backspace key** until everything you want to erase is gone

Notepad

The backspace key and the delete key differ from the arrow keys. Arrow keys allow you to move up, down, left or right within a document. They <u>do not change</u> or cause changes to be made to the document. If you are trying to make changes, the backspace and delete keys are developed to <u>**actually make changes**</u> in your document. The **delete** key will erase or delete text to the **right** of the cursor. The **backspace** key will erase or delete text to the **left** or backward direction of the cursor.

Highlight and Replace

1. Highlight or select the block of text you want to replace

2. Start to type the new text (you don't have to delete before you start typing).

3. As soon as you press the first key of the new text, the highlighted block will be deleted

4. As you type, the new text will be inserted

The Undo and Redo Button

- In case you mistakenly erase or delete a text or graphic, <u>don't panic</u>. Simply click on the **Undo** button, or choose **Edit → Undo,** or simply hold down the **Ctrl** key and press **Z.** This will only undo the last action or changes made to your document.

- **Undo** will work an unlimited number of times, recalling in sequence changes made to a document.

- If your actions are not made in error, always feel free to use the **Redo** button, or choose **Edit → Redo** or simply hold down the **Alt + Shift** and press **Backspace.**

Format Text Using **Bold** <u>Underline</u>, and *Italic*

- To **Bold,** first highlight the text you want to bold. Click on **B** button in the toolbars or simply hold down the **Ctrl** key and press **B.** You will be able to see the bolded text as soon as the highlight is removed.

- <u>To Underline a text,</u> highlight the text you want to underline. Click on <u>U</u> button in the toolbars or simply hold down the **Ctrl** key and press U.

- *To italicize a text,* highlight the text you want to italicize. Click on *I* button or simply hold down the **Ctrl** key and press *I.*

- **Remove Bold, <u>Underline,</u> and *Italics.*** You will basically have to do what you did to create the **Bold, <u>Underline,</u> and *Italics***

Using the Keyboard to highlight

There are so many reasons you will need to select (highlight) information. Perhaps you just want to replace information, change the character or paragraph format, copy, move , or delete information. As with most *Windows* applications, *Word* works on the "select, then move, replace or delete" principle. When you highlight an area, you are shifting focus into the highlighted area. Any action performed will only affect that area only.

Steps

1. Move the insertion point (cursor) to the beginning of the text you want to select.

2. Use one of the key combinations in the following tables to select the text.

Highlight Text Using the Arrow Keys

Key	Resulting Action
Shift + ↓ [Down arrow] or ↑ [Up arrow]	Highlight one line at a time
Shift + → [Right arrow] or Shift + ← [Left arrow]	Highlight one character at a time
Shift + Ctrl + → or Shift + Ctrl + ←	Highlight one word at a time
Shift + Ctrl + ↓ or Shift + Ctrl + ↑	Highlight one paragraph at a time

Highlight Text Using the Home and End Keys

Key	Resulting Action
Shift + Home	Highlight from the insertion point (cursor point) to the beginning of the current line
Shift + End	Highlight from the insertion point to the end of the current line
Shift + Ctrl + Home	Highlight from the insertion point to the beginning of the document
Shift + Ctrl + End	Highlight from the insertion point to the end of the document
Ctrl + A	Highlight the entire document, regardless of where the insertion point is

Other Useful Shortcuts

Keys	Resulting Action
Ctrl + L	Align Left
Ctrl + E	Center
Ctrl + R	Align Right
Ctrl + J	Justify
Ctrl + F	Find and Replace
Ctrl + G	Go to page, line, section, etc.
Ctrl + Backspace	Delete a word to the left
Ctrl + Y or simply press F4	Repeat your last action
Ctrl + Home	Go to the beginning of a document
Ctrl + End	Go to the end of a document
Shift + F7	Open the Thesaurus
Ctrl + K	Insert a hyperlink
Ctrl + Z	Undo
Alt + Shift + Backspace	Redo

We are now ready to edit our document. Move the cursor to the beginning of the second paragraph and highlight the entire paragraph. After that, click on the **Cut** button or choose **Edit → Cut**.

After that, move your cursor to the new location where you want to place the new text. In this case, move the cursor to two spaces below the following line:

"Photo identification"

Spell Check

1. Move the mouse pointer over to the misspelled word and right-click the mouse. Choose and click on the correct spelling, or

2. Choose <u>T</u>ools → <u>S</u>pelling and Grammar

3. When you see the correct spelling in the **Suggestions** box of the *Spelling and Grammar* window, click to select it and then click **Change** to make the correction.

4. Another way to correct your spelling error(s) is to move the mouse over to the misspelled word and **Right-click** the mouse. You will see a pop-up window showing what the correct spelling should be. Click on the correct spelling to accept, thereby correcting the error, or

5. You can correct the same spelling error quickly without checking the entire document using a much more faster and efficient way than the one stated in step 4 above. To find the next misspelled word in the document, press **Alt + F7**. You will see a pop-up window showing what the correct spelling should be, click on the correct spelling to accept.

Bullet and Numbering

Highlight the three items you are asking patients to bring next time they are coming to see their doctors. They are as following:

> Insurance card
> Social Security card, and
> Photo identification

Highlight all three and click **Numbering** button on the Standard toolbars, or simply choose **Format → Bullet and Numbering**. On the *Bullets and Numbering* window, click **Numbered** tab and select number format you like and then click **Ok**.

To Insert Date

1. Choose **Insert → Date and Time** and pick the date and time in the format of February 7, 2003. Or

2. Simply press **Alt + Shift + D**. This method will produce a date in this format: **3/24/2003**

To Insert Accent or Special Character such as ½, ©, č , à and more

1. Click where you want to insert the accent or character.
2. Choose **Insert → Symbol…** and when the following **Symbol** window pops up.

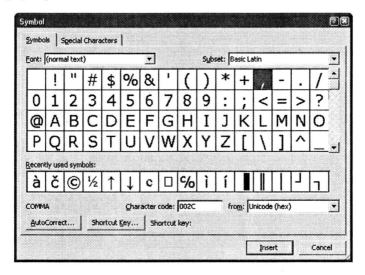

3. Scroll through it to pick the symbol of your choice.
4. Click Insert and then click Close.

Insert the symbol using the numeric keypad.

5. Simply complete step one and move on to step five
6. Make sure the **Num Lock** is on.
7. Hold down the **ALT** key, and then, using the numeric keypad, type the character code.

Here are some commonly used codes:

Word 2000 Codes	Word XP Codes	Result
Alt + Ctrl + C	Alt + Ctrl + C	©
171	0189	½
130	0224	À
129	0252	Ü

When you finish, your document should look like the following:

MidMed©

2449 Golf Road
Philadelphia, PA 19131
Voice (215) 555-1212
Fax (215) 555-6767

January 23, 2003

«Prefix» «First_Name» «Last_Name»
«Address_Line_1»
«Address_Line_2»
«City», «State» «ZIP_Code»

Dear «Prefix» «Last_Name»:

This is to remind you of your previously scheduled appointment with «Clinician» for Medication check on Thursday, January 29, 2003 at 10:30 am, and also with «Therapist» for psychotherapy at 11:00 am. You are hereby advised to arrive early. Your total time at the clinic is expected to be 1½ hours.

When coming, kindly remember to bring the following with you:

Insurance card
Social Security card; and
Photo identification

If you have any questions or concerns, or you are going to be late for whatever reasons, feel free to call me at (215) 999-6161 or call your Psychiatrist and Therapist directly. Their numbers are as following:

Sincerely,

Maria Villanueva
Secretary

cm
Enclosure
c: Front Desk Personnel

Going back to where you left off in Word Documents

Working on a long document can sometimes require that you stop to do something else such as look for more information or simply take a break. When this happens, it's easy to lose track of the exact page and paragraph where you left off. With Microsoft Word documents, picking up where you left off is very easy to do. It does not require special formatting or complicated steps. All you need to do is hold down the **Shift** key and press F5. The system will take you to where you were before you left to go grab a cup of coffee or make that important phone call. Don't forget, the magic is **Shift** + F5. Oh, one more thing, you can do the **Shift** + F5 until you reach the location you want out of your last two locations.

Let us save what we have done so far before moving on to something new. Make sure you save both the data source and your letter. If you are trying to exit Word and dialog window pops up asking "Do you want to save changes to 'database file name'", click **Yes** to save the data source and also click **Yes** to save your document.

CHAPTER FIVE

Internet Integration and Sending Fax

We need to have Ms. Jones review what we have done so far. As you know, Ms. Jones is very busy. It is impossible to have her come to the location where we are currently helping her Secretary to complete this project. Instead, we are going to send a copy of our letter to Ms. Jones for review and corrections (if any).

Make sure that the edited copy of the patient letter is up on your screen before completing the following steps. However, there are some issues to consider before we are ready to go ahead and send our file to Ms. Jones. First and foremost is the need to keep different versions of the same document. Why would we want to do that? One reason may be to be able to look back and see the evolution of our document. Another reason may be just to have different snapshots of our document moment by moment. Whatever the reason, we are going to save the copy we are about to send to Ms. Jones as our first version and when we receive a corrected copy back from Ms. Jones, we are going to save that one as another version. I want you to bear in mind that you can do this if you are writing a document longer than one page. You can do this if you are intending to write a book. To save our letter as a different version, follow the steps below:

Steps
1. Choose **File** → **Versions** and that should bring out the *Versions* window
2. Click **Save Now…** and when the *Save Version* window pops up.
3. Typing a comment in the **Comment on version** box is optional.
4. Click **Ok**.

We can now go ahead and send our document (or file) to Ms. Jones. We are going to send our document via e-mail as an attachment or via fax.

E-mail attachment steps

1. If you are not currently online, make sure you do so. It'll be very difficult to complete this without access to online (if you don't have access to online, don't worry about it. You can always come back to try this portion of the book). Not only that, make sure your Microsoft Outlook is running as either the default mail client or alternative mail client (this is necessary and required for a smooth collaboration). If your Microsoft Outlook is not configured as the default mail client, you are likely to receive the following warning:

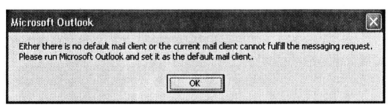

2. Choose **File** → **Send To** → **Mail Recipient (as Attachment)**. If you are using Microsoft Office XP, it is advisable to click on **Mail Recipient (for Review)**. And from the following window:

3. Type Ms. Jones' **e-mail address** in the input box across from **To:**

4. The body of your message should read "Please review the attached document." Always feel free to add more to this message if you have to. Otherwise, click **Send** to complete.

Creating and Sending a Fax

Microsoft Word 2000 as well as Microsoft Word XP includes features to help you create and send a fax. If your fax is already set up and the fax recipients are listed in your address book, you can use the Fax Wizard to look up the recipients' fax numbers. The Fax Wizard is 100% compatible with the following types of electronic address books:

- Microsoft Outlook Address Book or Contact List
- The Personal Address Book

If you have a fax program installed on your computer, you can use the Fax Wizard to create a cover sheet for the document you are about to fax and then send the cover sheet and the document from within Word.

To create and send a document and cover sheet

1. Make sure the document you want to send is currently active on your screen.

2. While the document is open, start the Fax Wizard and then choose **File → Send To,** and then click **Fax Recipient.**

The Fax Wizard leads you through the process of creating a cover sheet and then sending the cover sheet and your document.

Windows XP

If your computer is equipped with Windows XP, you may have to install **Fax Services** before you can send your document to Ms. Jones or to anyone else for that matter (unless it has been installed). To install **Fax Services,** follow the steps below but make sure you have your original Windows XP Professional CD as well as your Microsoft Office CD around just in case the system requests for either one or both.

To Install Fax Services in Windows XP

1. Click **Start → Control Panel → Add or Remove Programs.**

2. Look to right of the screen that pops up after you click on Add or Remove Programs and click on **Add/Remove Windows Components** and that should activate the following screen.

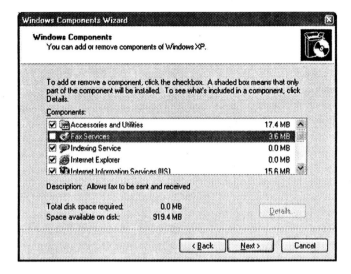

3. The fact that there is no check mark next to your **Fax Services** clearly indicates that the fax services have never been installed. If that is the case, click the check box next to **Fax Services** to select it, and then

4. Click **Next**. From this point on, carefully follow the Installation instructions on the screen. The system will no doubt ask you for your Windows XP CD and again for your Microsoft Office CD. It is advisable to have both ready.

5. When the installation of fax services is completed, and you see the following screen, click **Finish**.

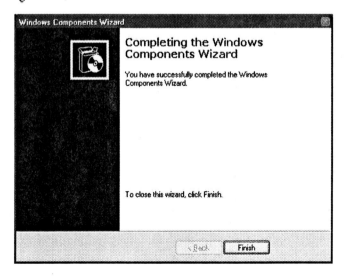

Now that your fax is installed, the next thing is to start using it. Let us go ahead and fax your document.

1. Choose **File** → **Print** and that should take you to the following print screen:

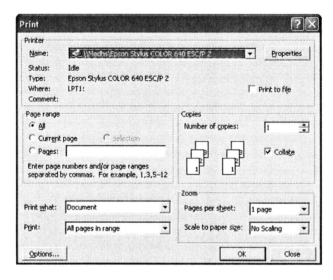

2. Click on the little box facing **Name:** to select your fax. After that, click **Ok**. The system should activate the following Send Fax Wizard.

3. Click **Next**. Please make sure you have the recipient information such as <u>Name</u>, <u>Fax Number</u>, and even the <u>Subject matter</u> of your fax message ready for the wizard to do a good job.

4. The **"Send Fax Wizard"** should lead you to the Fax Monitor screen. Click **More >>** to see the status of your fax. When the fax is completed, simply close the Fax Monitor.

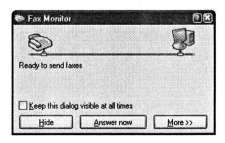

If Your Computer Does Not Support Faxing
You can use the Fax Wizard in Word 2000 to create and print cover sheets. You can then send the cover sheets and documents to recipients by using a stand alone fax machine.

To create and print a cover sheet, start the Fax Wizard
1. On the **File** menu, click **New.**
2. Click the **Letters and Faxes** tab.
3. Double-click the **Fax Wizard.**

Creating Envelopes—mail merge

Before we completely leave the subject of mail merge, there are two things we have to do. First, we need to create envelope and mailing labels for our mail merge. With the *Mail Merge Helper*, we can create mail merge envelopes and labels designed to use the same data source (database) as the letter we created.

We are going to use the data source created earlier. It just doesn't make sense to create a different data source.

 If you are using a Clinical Solution software that allows you to integrate with Microsoft Office, you do not need to create a separate data source or database from scratch.

Notepad

Steps
1. With the main document active, choose <u>T</u>ools → **Mail Merge.** Click the <u>C</u>reate button under <u>Step 1</u> Main Document, select <u>E</u>nvelopes, and then

select either the <u>A</u>ctive Window or <u>N</u>ew Main Document button. In this case, let us select **New Main Document** button.

2. Click the <u>G</u>et Data button under <u>Step 2</u> Data Source, and then select **<u>O</u>pen Data Source** to find the data source file. Select the file name "Patient Database" and choose **<u>O</u>pen**.

3. Click **<u>S</u>et Up Main Document** to display the Envelope Options dialog window. Select an **Envelope <u>S</u>ize**, and if necessary, change any of the other options. Choose **OK** to display the Envelope Address dialog window.

4. Insert the appropriate *merge fields* in the Sample Envelope Address text box using the **In<u>s</u>ert Merge Field** button. Choose the **Insert Postal <u>B</u>ar Code** if you want Word to insert the POSTNET bar code on the labels, then choose **OK**.

5. Proceed with the merge options under <u>Step 3</u> **Merge the Data with the Document**.

Creating Mailing Labels

If you don't want to print recipient names and addresses directly onto each envelop, mailing labels is another choice. You can design a form that prints multiple labels on a page similar to the way you design a form letter. Again, we are going to use the same data source for our mailing labels.

Steps

1. Choose <u>T</u>ools → Mail Merge. (Unlike other mail merges, the main form letter document does not need to be active.) Click the **<u>C</u>reate** button under <u>Step 1</u> Main Document, select **<u>M</u>ailing Labels**, and then select either the **<u>A</u>ctive Window** or **<u>N</u>ew Main Document** button. In this case, we are going to select **New Main Document** and then following the steps below.

2. Click the <u>G</u>et Data button under <u>Step 2</u> Data Source, and then select **<u>O</u>pen Data Source** to find the data source file. This step is necessary and required if you are going to use a different "Data Source." Select the file and choose **<u>O</u>pen**.

3. Click **<u>S</u>et Up Main** Document to display the **Label Options** dialog window. Select a label format from the **Product <u>N</u>umber** list box, and if necessary, change any of the other options. Choose **OK** to display the Create Labels dialog window.

4. Insert the appropriate *merge fields* in the Sample Label text box using the **Insert Merge Field** button. Use the **Insert Postal Bar Code** if you want Word to insert the POSTNET bar code on the labels, and then choose **OK**.

5. Proceed with the merge options under Step 3 **Merge the Data with the Document.**

Finding Records in mail merge

Why would you want to find a specific record? Perhaps the address of a patient has changed. Or perhaps you received a "Return to Sender" notice from your last mailing. There are so many reasons you would want to find specific records in your mail merge. Regardless, all you need to do to locate the record is follow these steps.

Steps

1. To go to the data source, you can do one of two things depending on where you are. With the main document open, choose the **Edit Data Source** button on the **Mail Merge** toolbar.

2. Or, from the Mail Merge Helper dialog window, choose **Edit** under Step 2 **Data Source** and then click **the file name.**

3. Choose the **Find** button to display the **Find in Field** dialog window.

4. In the **Find What** text box, type what you are searching for. In the **In Field** list box, select the field name that contains the information you are searching for.

5. Click the **Find First** button, examine the record, and then click the **Find Next** button to continue the search. Choose **Close** when you are finished searching.

6. When you get to the record you need to edit, move through the *Data Form* fields by pressing the **Enter** or **Tab** or **Shift + Tab** keys. Click **OK** when you have finished editing information.

Merging Document with Data Source

Once you have created your main document and entered necessary information into your *Data Source* (Database), and you are ready to merge the two together, always make sure the letter or document you want to merge is currently active on your screen.

Steps

1. Choose **Tools** → **Mail Merge.**

2. When you get to the **Mail Merge Helper,** click **Merge** under **Merge the data with the document.** The following screen pops up.

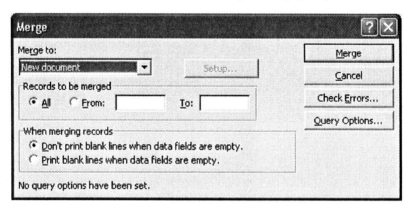

3. Under **Merge to:** click and select **New Document.** This will create a merged document in a new Word document with the temporary name Form Letters1, or

4. If you click **Merge to Printer.** The system will create the merged document and prints it on the currently selected printer.

5. The next step is to make a selection under **Records to be merged.** If you click **All,** this will merge the letter as per information in your data source or database. When you click **From** the system will let you type the appropriate number corresponding to the record you want to print. Always remember to clearly state **From** and **To**

6. Under **When merging records** always make sure that the radio button next to **Don't print blank lines when data fields are empty** is selected.

For more information on "Merging document with data source," go to www.mednetservices.com

CHAPTER SIX

Understanding Toolbars

Toolbars are more like mouse shortcuts to most program features. In addition to the **Standard** toolbars, there are in excess of 15 additional toolbars in *Word 2000* and over 20 additional toolbars in *Word XP* that you can use to quickly access most of *Microsoft Word* features. Like the menu in *Word 2000 and XP*, toolbars are also adaptive and may change depending on how often you use them.

Creating a New Toolbar

You may want to create your own custom toolbar showing only the buttons required for the specific tasks that you frequently perform. If you use a document that has unique formatting and perhaps printing requirements such as the mail merge document we just created, you can create a new toolbar with just those buttons to avoid having to go through the long and sometime time consuming steps.

Steps

1. **Right-click** any toolbar, then choose **C**ustomize. Or click **T**ools → **C**ustomize. Either way should lead you to the **Customize** screen which shows the following three tabs: "Toolbars," "Commands," and "Options." Click the **Toolbars** tab.

2. Choose **N**ew button and that should activate the following screen:

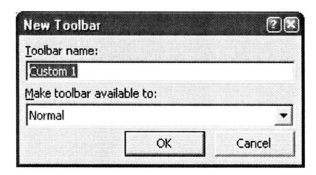

3. In the <u>T</u>oolbar Name text box, type *"My Office"* without the quotation marks as the name of your new toolbar; then click **Ok**.

4. Scroll down the list of toolbars in the **Toolbar** tab and you should see the new toolbar you just created.

Very soon I'm going to show you how to create new buttons to help you access your document and data source (database) faster than ever before. However, to add any of the existing buttons such as the **Save All** and **Close All** to the new toolbar you just created (this way you will not have to hold down **Shift** key when you click on **File** to activate those hiding menu options) follow these steps:

5. To add any of the existing buttons to your new toolbar, click the <u>C</u>ommands tab in the **Customize** dialog window.

6. In the **Categories** list box, select the category that includes the command you want the button to perform—in this case, click on **File**. Find the button that says *"Save All"* in the **Comman<u>d</u>s** list, and then **drag** that button to the new toolbar. Release the mouse button.

7. **Repeat Step 4** for each additional button such as *"Close All"* you want to add to the new toolbar. Your new toolbar will expand as you continue to add buttons. When you are finished, click **Close**.

After you create a new toolbar, you can move or resize it just as you can move or resize Word's predefined toolbars.

Displaying or Hiding Toolbars

When you start Word, by default, the Standard and Formatting toolbars are the only toolbars likely to appear on your screen. The general consensus is that no matter what, you are bound to use these toolbars when you work in Word. There are several additional toolbars you can display when you need them. Sometimes, different toolbars will automatically appear on-screen when you are performing certain procedures. For example, when you are recording Macro, the Stop Recording toolbar appears on-screen. To help you identify which toolbar(s) are currently displayed on-screen, when you click <u>V</u>iew, and then <u>T</u>oolbars you will see a check mark next to each toolbar currently on-screen.

The choice to display more than the Standard and Formatting toolbars is entirely up to the individual user. Once a toolbar is activated, you can move it to virtually any location but it is much more logical to keep them well organized around the Standard toolbars which are located underneath your main menus. To display each toolbar, follow these steps:

1. Click **View → Toolbars** and this will bring up the list of available toolbars. Pick one-by-one those you will like to display up on your screen, or

2. Move your mouse to the toolbar area and **Right-click** the mouse on any toolbar, and then click **the name of the toolbar** you want to display.

To hide a toolbar

1. Click **View → Toolbars.** Clicking on the toolbar you want to hide will remove the previously placed check mark thereby taking it out of view, or

2. **Right-click any toolbar,** then click **the name of the toolbar** you want to hide.

 If the toolbar is a floating toolbar, you can hide it by clicking the **Close** button in the toolbar's title bar.

Adding Toolbar Buttons

If you frequently use a command that is not represented on a Word toolbar, you can easily add a button to a toolbar that performs the command. If there is no room to add a button to an existing toolbar, you can remove an existing button on a toolbar that you don't use or you can create a new toolbar.

Steps

1. Display the toolbar that you want to add a button to, if necessary.
2. Choose **Tools** → **Customize**; then click the **Commands** tab.
3. In the Categories list box, select the category that includes the command you want the button to perform.
4. Find the button you want in the **Commands** list, and then **drag** that button to where you want the toolbar button to appear on the displayed toolbar. Release the mouse button.
5. Click **Close** to close the Customize dialog window.

Notepad

To remove a button from a toolbar, display the toolbar that includes the button you want to remove. Choose **Tools** → **Customize**; then click the **Commands** tab. **Drag** the button off the toolbar; then click **Close**. To reset a toolbar to its original configuration, choose **Tools** → **Customize**; then click the **Toolbars** tab. Select the toolbar you want to reset, and then click the **Reset** button. Click **Ok** to confirm the procedure; then click **Close** to close the dialog window.

CHAPTER SEVEN

Recording Macro—the beginning of automation

There are some tasks that are just too long and at times too technical to repeat over and again. In a busy environment, such a lengthy and highly involved task may often-times result in human error unless something is done to reduce the possibility of unnecessary mistakes.

Any environment where employees are overworked and underpaid will surely lead to low morale and high rate of turnover. It appears that the programmers behind the development of Microsoft Office are not unaware of this fact. They are also aware of the fact that having too many people on the same assignment can at times lead to unnecessary duplications that if not properly handled in a professional way can lead to personality clashes.

In order to make the work environment less intimidating, less conflicting and error-prone, we are going to employ the use of macro to help us accomplish some of these tasks effectively and efficiently without making too much demand on anyone's time and expertise. Macro provides a means to create mini-automation without getting into all the nitty-gritty of programming. A macro provides a way to record a set of instructions that can be played back at a later time. Word's macro is capable of recording keystrokes and any associated command necessary to perform a task.

If playing back the macro results in another lengthy step, what good is it? A macro should be designed to save time and effort, thereby increasing productivity. We are going to learn the steps necessary to record macro, assign that macro to a keystroke and the same keystroke to an object like a toolbar button we can click in order to make playing it back as smooth as it can possibly be.

Recording Macros

Please bear in mind that our goal is to find a way to reduce the number of steps required to access what we have created so far. Needless to say, we went through a lot of steps to create our data source but do we really need to go through the same long steps just to add more information to the same data source? Not if we can avoid it. If that is the case, I'm going to show you how we can program everything into a toolbar button. Did I just mention program? I did not mean to scare you in any way, shape, or form. However, there is a program included with your Microsoft Office known as Visual Basic for Application (VBA). Believe it or not, there is no better way to automate or customize program features in Microsoft Office. But when the time comes I will expose you to the beauty of VBA. As you will soon discover when you record a macro in Word or any program, you are in a way creating a Visual Basic for Application module with programming instructions. I'm not going to go into something I am not really ready to cover because of the fact that the subject of VBA is beyond the scope of this book. For now, let's go ahead and deal graciously with the subject before us and that is recording macros.

Before you perform the following steps, make sure the mail merge letter you created earlier is opened and active on your computer screen.

Steps

1. Choose <u>T</u>ools → <u>M</u>acro → <u>R</u>ecord New Macro. In the <u>M</u>acro Name text box, type a name for the macro.

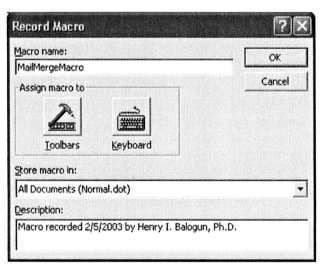

2. In the **Store Macro In** box, click to select the location where you want to store the macro. If you want a macro to be available whenever you use Word, select the **All Documents (Normal.dot)** option.

3. First of all, to assign a shortcut key to the macro, click the **Keyboard** button and that should activate the following screen:

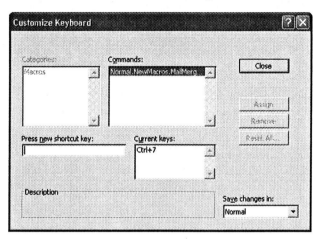

4. Make sure your cursor is blinking in the box labeled **Press New Shortcut Key**. Hold down **Alt**, or **Ctrl** key and press a letter or any number. For the sake of our project, let us hold down the **Ctrl** key and press 7. Our shortcut should read **Ctrl + 7** in the **Press New Shortcut Key** box. The inscription beneath it should read "Currently assigned to [unassigned]." If it doesn't, try another combination until it reads "Currently assigned to [unassigned]."

5. Click the **Assign** button followed by **Close** button.

6. Now we are going to perform the actions we want the macro to record and they are the following:

   a. Choose **Tools → Mail Merge**

   b. Under Step 2, click on **Edit** and when the name of your mail merge data source appears under **Edit**, click on the name

   c. When the **Data Form** screen appears, click **Ok**.

7. To stop recording, look for the following hanging toolbar:

8. Click on the **Stop Recording** button on the toolbar.

Running Macro

Once you have created a macro, running it is easy. When we were recording the last macro, we assigned the macro to a shortcut—Ctrl + 7. To run the macro, make sure the original mail merge letter is open and active on your screen.

Hold down the **Ctrl** key and press **7**. The Data Form screen should pop up. To run a macro from the **Tools** menu, follow these steps:

1. Open the document in which you want to run the macro—in this case, open the mail merge letter

2. Choose **Tools** → **Macro** → **Macros**.

3. In the list box, select the macro you want to run; then click **Run** to run the macro.

Assigning a Macro to a Button

Once you have created a macro to automate repetitive tasks, you can assign the macro to a button on the toolbar to make it much easier to use.

Steps

1. Display the toolbar that you want to add the button to. We are going to add the new button to the toolbar we created earlier. Don't forget that we gave the new toolbar the name "My Office."

2. **Right-click** on the toolbars of your choice, then choose **Customize** from the shortcut menu.

3. In the **Categories** list box, select **Macros**. In the **Commands** list, find the macro you want to place on the toolbar, and then drag that new macro name to your new toolbar. Release the mouse button.

4. To change the macro name you just dragged onto your new toolbar button, right-click the name. **Do not** close the **Customize** dialog window while you are doing this. Then, in the **Name** text box, type or edit the name; right-click the button again and point to the **Change Button Image** command to choose an image from the displayed choices.

5. If you want to display just the image, right-click the button and select **Default Style**. Click **Close** to close the Customize dialog window.

Feel free to visit www.mednetservices.com for lots of free downloadable files including extensive information and instructions on Recording Macro and also on Assigning a Macro to a Button and more.

Protecting Office Documents from Macro Viruses

In these days of unexpected computer viruses, one thing you seriously don't need is the one generated by the system itself either through the use of program features or conflict in applications. It is always good to know how to protect your documents from macro viruses simply by selecting an appropriate security level.

A macro virus can occur when "the macro picked up some harmful codes written in the macro language of programs" as a result of inappropriate recording of macros or when the macro is inadvertently altered. Just like any other virus out there, these viruses can do serious harm to programs and data.

To protect your document or data in Microsoft Word, Excel, and PowerPoint, it is advisable to set the security level to low, medium or high. If you fail to protect your document, Microsoft Office automatically disables macros without notice and this may render the macro you recorded ineffective.

Level of Protection

By default, Excel and PowerPoint are set to the medium security level, and Word is set to the "high" security level. Always remember to set the appropriate security level for your system.

1. **Low Security:** "When the security level is set to low, Office performs no macro checking when you open a document and enables all macros. This security level is not recommended because no protection is active when it is selected."

2. **Medium Security:** "When the security level is set to medium, you are prompted to enable or disable macros in documents when you open the documents. It is recommended that you disable a macro if you do not know who created it."

3. **High Security:** "When the security level is set to high, macros must have digital identification stamps indicating that the macros have not been altered. Otherwise, when you open a document, Office automatically disables macros without notice."

To set a security level for your computer

1. Choose **Tools** → **Macro**, and then click **Security**.

2. Click the **Security Level** tab, and then click the radio button next to a security level you prefer.

Notepad

For more information about how you can protect documents from macro viruses, go to www.mednetservices.com for lots of free downloadable files. If the file you are looking for is not available right away, all you need to do is come back again as we are constantly adding more files everyday.

For more information about how you can protect documents from macro viruses, go to www.mednetservices.com for lots of free downloadable files. If the file you are looking for is not available right away, all you need to do is come back again as we are constantly adding more files everyday.

Create Easy Access to Documents You Use Often

At times you need to dig deeper to find a better way to make things easier on yourself. It is easy to create a file and not remember where that file is in your system. In order to eliminate unnecessary frustration and headache, there is an option known as **Work** menu in Word that only few people know about. You can use this feature to keep an easily accessible list of your favorite Word files. This is like creating a shortcut. Your current menu options are:

File	Edit	View	Insert	Format	Tools	Table	Window	Help

We are going to add the **Work** menu to the menu bar. But before you do that, make sure there are no files currently open. It is advisable to do this the moment you start Microsoft Word.

Steps

1. On the **Tools** menu, click **Customize**, and then click the **Commands** tab.

2. In the **Categories** box, click **Built-in Menus**.

3. Click **Work** in the **Commands** box and drag it next to the Help menu.

Now that you have the Work menu in place, you can add any open Word document to your list. Let us go ahead and open the document we created earlier. Follow the steps outlined below:

1. To add the current document to the Work menu, on the **Work** menu, click **Add to Work Menu.**

2. To open a document, on the **Work** menu, click the document you want to open.

If you mistakenly add a document to your **Work** menu and you have to remove it for any reason, follow these steps to remove the document.

1. Press **Ctrl + ALT +**—(dash key). Your cursor will look like a large, bold underscore.

2. Click to activate **Work** menu, and

3. On the **Work** menu, click the document you want to remove.

CHAPTER EIGHT

Document Design and Translation

We have a feedback from the Clinical Director. Needless to say, she is very grateful for taking the time to help her Secretary in the effort to accomplish her goal. However, there are some new requests. She would like to know if it is possible to:

1. Include a table in the letter. The table should be designed to show Names, Availability and Phone Numbers of every Psychiatrist and Therapist per patient (this is indicated in the comment she inserted in the letter she sent back to us).

2. Design Business Card for every Psychiatrist and Therapist

3. Design a new:

   a. Consent to treatment

   b. Patient right

   c. Psychiatric Evaluation Form

   d. Release of Information

4. Translate every document including the letter we created a while ago, into Spanish.

Before you run undercover or take the next flight out of town, I just want to let you know that you can actually do all these using your Microsoft Word. I'm going to show you how to accomplish it in just a few minutes.
I don't want you to dwell on the illusion that once the handshake has taken place, our job is done. If anything, the handshake means that the work has just begun. But for now, let us concentrate on the task before us.

Dealing with Comment

Let me explain briefly the use of comment in Microsoft Word. In addition to the e-mail message received from the Clinical Director, she also sent back the same letter we sent to her for review. On the letter she indicated through the use of comment the precise location where changes should be made. This requires explanation as to how to use comment in Microsoft Word.

A comment is a text note that you can embed inside a Word document to indicate what changes are required and where the changes are to be made or should go. One good thing about Word comment is its ability to display, separately, the name of the author as well as the text of the comment. The following is a copy of the letter with a comment as to where we should insert table:

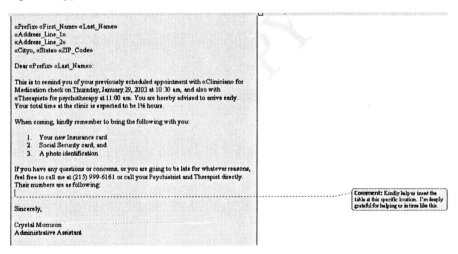

Insert a comment

1. Click the location where you want to place comment.
2. On the **Insert** menu, click **Comment**.
3. Type the comment text in the **comment balloon.**
4. In case the comment balloon is not displayed, type the comment in the **Reviewing Pane**
5. To view the name of the reviewer, move your mouse over the comment and it should display the name of the reviewer.

To respond to a comment

1. Click the existing comment, choose **Insert → Comment.**

2. Type your response in the new **comment balloon**

To delete (remove) a comment

1. Move your mouse on the comment you want to delete and right-click the mouse

2. On the pop up menu, click **Delete comment**

We can now go ahead to attend to the Director's request by starting with the creation and printing of a business card. Some of the ways you can create attractive and professional business card quickly using *Microsoft Word 2000 or Word XP (2002)* is to either use ready-made business card templates from the Microsoft Office Template Gallery, or create one from scratch with the help of the **Envelopes and Labels** dialog window. I'm going to show you how to create one from scratch.

Create and print business cards

1. From Word 2000, choose **Tools → Envelopes and Labels** (if you are using Word XP, choose **Tools → Letters and Mailings** and then click **Envelopes and Labels**). Either one should take you to the following screen:

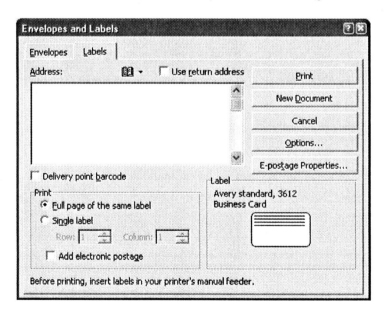

2. Click the **Labels** tab, and in the **Address** box, enter the following information about one of the Psychotherapists. Also, don't forget to enter the name of the clinic and phone number. In other word, enter the following information exactly as you see it:

MidMed©
Mari Fukushima, MA
Psychotherapist
2449 Golf Road
Philadelphia, PA 19131
Voice (215) 555-1212
Fax (215) 555-6767

3. Under **Print,** do not change the selected default which is **Full page of the same label.** This allows you to print multiple business cards on a perforated, heavyweight cardstock sheet by *Avery.*

4. Click **Options,** and the **Label Options** screen pops up,

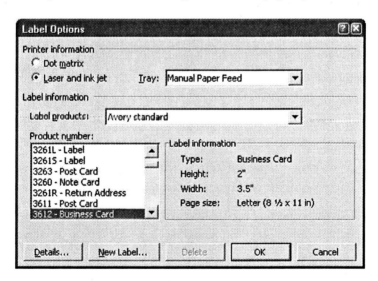

5. Click one of the radio buttons under **Printer information** to choose between **Dot matrix** or **Laser and Ink Jet** printer (whichever one you prefer—I'm quite sure your choice will be **Laser and Ink Jet**).

6. In **Label products** under **Label Information,** leave the default selected, **Avery Standard.**

7. Under **Product number,** choose the business card number corresponding to the Avery Product you are going to use. In our case, click **3612 Business Card.** Just in case the product number you want is not listed, one of the listed labels may correspond to the paper size you want. Watch out for the number as well as the paper size under **Label Information.**

8. Click **Ok.**

9. You are now back in the **Envelopes and Labels** dialog window.

10. To modify the business card, click **New Document**

11. Highlight the clinic name, choose **Format → Font,** and on the Font window are the following tabs: *Tab, Character Spacing* and *Text Effects* (Word XP)

12. With the **Font** tab activated, choose **Times New Roman** under **Font,** and make the **Font Style** = Bold and **Font Size** = 18, and click **Ok.**

13. After that, highlight the name and title of the Psychotherapist, and choose **Format → Font** to make the following changes. **Font** = Times New Roman, **Font Style** = Regular, **Font Size** = 11

14. Click **Ok.** While the name and title is still highlighted, click **Align Right** button on the **Formatting** toolbar or simply hold down the **Ctrl** and press **R**

15. Do the same to the address of the clinic but **Align Left.** Your business card should look like the following:

MidMed©

Mari Fukushima, MA
Psychotherapist

2449 Golf Road
Philadelphia, PA 19131
Voice (215) 555-1212
Fax (215) 555-6767

16. Copy cell one to all the 10 cells of your business card page but make sure you limit everything to only one page.

> **To copy from one cell and paste to another:**
>
> Move the mouse close to **the edge** of the cell you just formatted. Your mouse will appear like this =>. Move the mouse on to the edge of the line of the cell and it will change to a small solid dark arrow. When you see the solid dark arrow, click the cell to highlight it. Hold down **Ctrl** key and press **C** to copy. To paste, press the **Tab** key to move and highlight the next cell. When the next cell is highlighted, hold down the **Ctrl** key and press **V**.

17. To print your business card, load the Avery Business Card paper into your printer

18. Choose **File → Print**. Make sure your printer's name is displayed in the **Printer Name** box and click **Ok**. (More on printing document later on)

I'm quite sure you can do a better design of business card than the one we did together. Experiment and practice as much as you can, and don't forget to visit www.mednetservices.com to download some Business Card templates you can use over and again.

Translate Word Document from inside Word

Translating a word, phrase or even an entire document into another language is easy to do in Microsoft Word XP than in Word 2000. This is a goal that can be accomplished by using the **Translate** task pane (available only in Word XP otherwise known as Word 2002). Not only does this provide access to many languages now available in Word, you can also use it to access the appropriate online site where you do most of your language translations effortlessly.

For those of you who are using Word XP, on the **Tools** menu point to **Language** and click **Translate**. This will activate the **Language task pane** to the right of your screen like the one below:

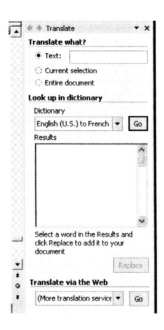

You should be able to see the task pane open to the right of your screen. From this task pane, you can:

1. Check words or phrases in the dictionary of another language, provided that the language dictionary is installed in your computer system.

2. Use the **Translate** task pane to insert translated text directly into your document.

3. Use the **Translate** task pane to access translation services on the World Wide Web, to translate a section of text or an entire document.

4. Click the **Go** button under **Translate via the Web** to translate text. You've got to be online (on the Internet) to enjoy this service.

If this is your first time using the language translator via Microsoft Word, the system will take you to the Internet site where you can install an appropriate language translator of your choice. When you click **Go**, you should see a web page showing the map of different Microsoft locations around the world. Click on the **Country** where you are and that will direct you to the appropriate web page where you can install the language translator of your choice.

5. The title of the next page should say, **Translate Within Word**

6. Pick one of the two plug-in translators currently available for Word XP (2002) to download and install. Depending on the speed of your system, downloading should not take longer than a few seconds. After the download, install the plug-in (program) right away. To use it, follow these simple steps:

   a. From your Microsoft Word, choose **Tools → Language → Translate**.

   b. You've got to be online to use the program

   c. Highlight the area of your document to translate

   d. Click the box under **Translate via the Web** in the **Translate** task pane.

   e. Pick a language of your choice. Example: **English (US) to Spanish (Spain)**

   f. Click **Go** and the translation begins. When you see the correct translation of your text, don't just sit there and enjoy it all alone, pick up the phone and

7. Call me in the morning and let me know that this is the best thing since sliced bread. (I'm just kidding. Don't go looking for my phone number—I don't have one).

Notepad

Ordinarily, most languages (other than English—USA and Western European) are not part of the standard installation of Microsoft Word. However, if you are going to use another language, it is advisable to install one of the two available plug-in translators for Microsoft Word XP (2002). To install language translator, follow the instruction given earlier on the previous page. If you are using Word 2000, once your document is finished and ready to be translated, use the following site (among others) for the translation: http://www.worldlingo.com/microsoft/computer_translation.html

Before leaving the subject of language translation, I would like to give you your first and only homework. Let's see if you can translate this Yoruba language expression into English, Spanish, French and Japanese. The expression is "**Mo feran re.**" Send your response to Balogun@mednetservices.com . This is a homework assignment strictly for non-Yorubas. Yoruba speaking people are not eligible to participate. One more thing, if you can include the history (not detailed history) and culture of one of the most highly intelligent, loving and caring people on earth—the people of Ekiti, you will not only be my number one friend in the world, you will definitely win a surprise package. Good luck!

Create Tables

When it comes to organizing and formatting text and numbers or even graphics, tables are your number one means of doing it. Tables are one of Microsoft Word's most powerful and useful tools. You can use it to write movie scripts, resumes and advertising scripts. As a matter of fact, once you know how to create tables, there is no limit to what you can use it for. Tables are composed of cells like in Excel. These cells are organized in vertical columns and horizontal rows. Once a table is created, you can insert, edit, align, change line spacing, apply bullets and numbering and format your text or numbers any way you so desire. In a way, you can work within tables just as you would in a normal document.

How to create tables

1. You can use the **Insert Table** button available on the **Standard Toolbar,** or

2. Choose Insert → Tables. *Highlight the number of rows and columns* you want and simply **click,** or

3. You can create tables in Microsoft Word by simply typing out a string of **Plus Signs** (+) and **Minus Signs** (-). For example: When you type it exactly as you see it here; +————————————+———————— ——————-+———————————————+ and press **Enter,** you should have a table consisting of one row and three columns that looks like the following:

Notepad

If you are having problems with the third step explained above, don't panic. It could be that the feature that would have made it easier for you to perform this step is not yet turned on. All you need to do is turn on this important feature in Word. To do this, choose **Tools → AutoCorrect** (in Word XP, it is **AutoCorrect Options**). Then, click the **AutoFormat As You Type** tab and place a check mark in the **Tables** box.

To add more rows and delete row(s)

1. Simply move your cursor to the last column of the last row (if you have more than one row) and then press the **Tab** key, or

2. Move your cursor to the end of the last row and press the **Enter** key.

3. To delete row, place the cursor in the row you want to delete, choose Table → Delete → Row.

To add and delete columns

1. Move your cursor to where you want to add a column. Choose **Table → Insert,** and click on **Column to the left** or **Column to the right** depending on where you want to insert the new column.

2. In Word 2000, choose **Insert → Table** and then click **Add Colums.** To delete a column, move the cursor to the column you want to delete and choose **Table → Delete → Column.**

Before we forget, let us insert a table in the letter we created earlier. At the end of the last paragraph (the paragraph be "Sincerely"), press the **Enter** key twice. After that, try one of the steps for inserting a table explained above. Insert a table consisting of three rows and three columns. Type the heading and insert merge fields as follows:

First Row:	Staff	Availability	Phone Number
Second Row:	«Clinician»	«ClinAvailability»	«ClinPhoneNumber»
Third Row:	«Therapist»	«TherpAvailability»	«TherpPhoneNumber»

Dear «Prefix» «Last_Name»:

This is to remind you of your previously scheduled appointment with «Clinician» for Medication check on Thursday, January 29, 2003 at 10:30 am, and also with «Therapist» for psychotherapy at 11:00 am. You are hereby advised to arrive early. Your total time at the clinic is expected to be 1½ hours.

When coming, kindly remember to bring the following with you:

1. Insurance card
2. Social Security card; and
3. Photo identification

If you have any questions or concerns, or you are going to be late for whatever reasons, feel free to call me at (215) 999-6161 or call your Psychiatrist and Therapist directly. Their numbers are as following:

Staff	Availability	Phone Number
«Clinician»	«ClinAvailability»	«ClinPhoneNumber»
«Therapist»	«TherpAvailability»	«TherpPhoneNumber»

Sincerely,

Maria Villanueva
Secretary

cm
Enclosure
c: Front Desk Personnel

Formatting a Table

You can format a table basically the same way you format any text—change text color, font size, and background including line spacing. We are going to format the table we just inserted into the letter. To accomplish this goal, let us:

1. Click and place the cursor in the heading row—column one of row one.

2. Hold down the **Shift** key and press the **Right Arrow** key on your keyboard until the entire row is highlighted.

3. Choose **Format → Borders and Shading…** And that will take you to the following screen:

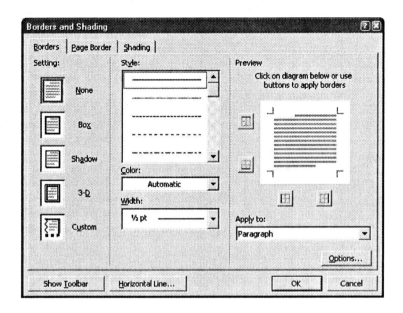

4. Click the **Shading** tab and from the forth row in the color palette, click the third column and the little box next to it should read **Olive Green** and click **Ok**.

5. While the heading is still highlighted, choose **Format → Font** and from the **Font Color**, click the last column of the last row which is **White**.

6. From the **Font Style**, click **Bold** and after that, click **Ok**.

7. To remove the highlight, press any **Arrow** key on your keyboard. After performing **Merge**, your table should look exactly like the following:

Staff	Availability	Phone Number
H. Desmond, MD	M – F (9:00 – 4:00)	215-777-9191
M. Sukukowa, MA	M – F (9:00 – 7:00)	215-777-8282

To adjust row heights and column widths

Position the mouse pointer on the gridline between columns and drag to the left to reduce the column or to the right to increase the column.

Wrap Text Around Tables

Word 2000 as well as Word XP provides new ways to wrap text around tables to create a professional looking document (I dare you to create one better than the one displayed here).

Staff	Availability	Phone Number
Dr. H. Desmond	M – F (9:00 – 4:00)	215-777-9191
M. Sukukowa	M – F (9:00 – 7:00)	215-777-8282

"Text automatically wraps around a table when you insert it on the left or right margin in a document with existing text." Bear in mind that a table that spread from left margin to the right margin will not work well with text wrap. The size of your table matters a great deal when it comes to wrapping text around tables.

To wrap text around a table

1. Click anywhere in the table. Choose **Table** → **Table Properties** or **Right click** on the table itself and then click **Table Properties**. Either way, when the following screen pops up

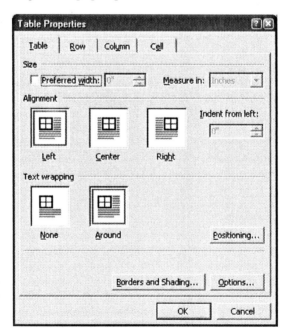

2. Click the **Table** tab. And under **Text wrapping,** click **Around.**

3. Click **Ok.**

More on this at www.mednetservices.com

Perform Calculations in a Table

Microsoft Word makes it possible to add, subtract, multiply, and divide values in table cells. One thing you really need to understand is how cells are referenced. In Microsoft Word individual table cells are referred to by the column letter and row number. Example, "A1" refers to the first column and first row while "B1" refers to the second column of the first row (just like in Excel). Let us create a table consisting of three rows and four columns table and populate the table like the one below:

256	584	217	1057
460	12	10	46
754	15	21	11310

To perform calculations

1. Make sure your cursor (the insertion point) is in cell A4 and that is column "A4" of the first row.

2. Choose **Table → Formula.** That will activate the calculation screen like the one below:

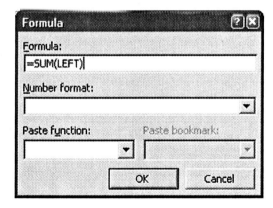

3. Under **Formula,** delete part of the automated formula. Delete the closing parenthesis and the word **Left** using backspace.

4. After the opening parenthesis, type this formula (A1:C1). When you are done, your formula should look exactly like =Sum(A1:C1)

5. Click **Ok.**

6. Move your cursor to column "D2" and choose **Table → Formula** and type the =A2/C2

7. Click **Ok.**

8. Move your cursor to column "D3" and repeat the rest of step 6 and then type =(A3)*B2

9. Click **Ok.** Your table should have the exact same numbers as the one shown below:

256	584	217	1057
460	12	10	46
754	15	21	11310

Some other formulas you can perform within tables in Microsoft Word:

Addition	=(A1)+16 or =(A1+A3)
Add a range of cells	=Sum(A1:C3)
Division	=(A2)/(C2) or =(A2)/10
Subtract two cells	=(A2-B2)
Multiplications	=(B1*B3) or =PRODUCT(B1)*(B3)

Notepad

Calculations in Microsoft Word do not necessarily work like calculations in Excel. If you add a row or column into the table you will have to manually recalculate or redefine your Word table formula. You are better off using Microsoft Excel to perform complex calculations. For more information and free downloads, go to www.mednetservices.com

CHAPTER NINE

Document Layout

In business, to say that image can sometimes make or break a business is nothing short of absolute truth. And when this basic principle is violated businesses are in a way playing the game of hit or miss with the possibility of a high risk of financial loss in the face of diminishing growth.

As you know, the goals of MidMed include increasing productivity and reducing idle time, which would eventually lead to increase in the bottom line. As for the Director, having any outside professional or consultant come in to help in time like this is unacceptable. We are going to focus our time and energy doing one thing and that is to help Ms. Jones' Secretary.

We have three important documents to prepare (Consent to Treatment, Release of Information and Patients' Right) and we cannot afford not to do a good job. Go to www.mednetservices.com to download copies. I want you to reproduce a better copy. This clinic is well known for its professionalism, and well organized environment. This is an image we are not prepared to trade for anything less the best.

The fact of the matter is that you are going to actually produce those documents. Hey, this is nothing to sneeze about. I'm going to give you an in-depth training in design and what goes into every aspect of creating professional looking documents. First of all, let us begin by looking into:

Page Setup

Changing Margins

There is no easier way to understand page setup without recalling its properties. As you will discover, the default settings are usually one-inch top and one-inch bottom margins. Another thing is the right and left margin which by default are set at 1.25" each.

Normally, the gutter margin is zero by default, and the header and footer from the edge is one-half inch. These settings are adequate for most documents but there are some instances whereby changing any of them is imperative. Changes made because of the requirement of one document do not change the default for every document. You have the option to change these default settings on a document-by-document basis, or change them permanently. The latter is not advisable in an environment like an outpatient clinic where producing different types of documents is highly required. To change the default settings, follow these steps:

1. Choose **File →**, **Page Setup**, and that should activate the **Page Setup** properties screen.

2. Click the **Margins** tab.

3. Under Margins feel free to **increase or decrease "Top," "Bottom," "Left," or "Right"** margins. Keep an eye on the **Preview** screen to see how the margins increase or decrease.

4. Set the **Header** and **Footer** as you please. The default is usually 0.5."

5. If you will be binding the document and want the inside margin to remain constant, click **Mirror Margins.** In Word XP, under **Paper** click the box next to **Multiple Pages** to select **Mirror Margins** in order to toggle that feature on and off.

6. In the **Apply To** box, indicate what section of the document you want these changes to affect (apply).

7. If you are creating a template and you want these changes to be available to all new documents using the same template, click **Default**, and then click **Yes.**

8. Click **Ok.**

Changing Paper Size

Steps

1. Choose **File → Page Set<u>u</u>p,** and then click the **Paper <u>S</u>ize** tab. If you are using Word XP, it is simply **Paper** tab.

2. Look for and select the paper size that matches your needs from the **Pape<u>r</u> Size** box.

3. If you cannot find your paper size in the **Paper Size** box, you can always type in the correct size in the **<u>W</u>idth** and **H<u>e</u>ight** text boxes. Or you can simply scroll through and select sizes of your choice.

4. To pick the appropriate orientation, in **<u>A</u>pply To** box, indicate what section of the document you want these changes to affect (apply).

5. If you are creating a template and you want these changes to be in effect with all new documents using the same template, click **<u>D</u>efault,** and then click **<u>Y</u>es.**

6. Click **Ok.**

Changing Paper Source

Steps

1. Choose **File → Page Set<u>u</u>p** to display the **Page Setup** dialog window as shown on the previous page.

2. From the dialog window, select the **<u>P</u>aper Source** tab.

3. Under the **<u>F</u>irst Page** list box, select the location for the paper of the first page of each document you are likely to print. It is advisable to leave this at the default setting.

4. Under the **<u>O</u>ther Pages** list box, select the location for the paper of the remaining pages you are likely to print. Again, it is advisable to leave this at the default setting.

5. In the **<u>A</u>pply To** box, indicate what section of the document you want these changes to affect (apply).

Changing Page Layout

If you are going to be using headers and footers, this will enable you to choose whether your headers and footers are the same all throughout the document you are creating, or change as you desire. Example: You can choose to print the header and footer on all pages except the first page. Not only that, you can also specify how you want text positioned on the page. To configure the page lay-out, follow these steps:

1. Choose **File → Page Setup** to display the Page Setup dialog window, and then click the **Layout** tab.

2. Under the **Section Start** drop-down list, select where you want the new section(s) to start.

3. In the radio button next to Headers and Footers section, click the options of your choice out of the only two available: **Different Odd and Even** or **Different First Page**.

4. Under **Vertical Alignment** drop-down arrow, click to choose between **Top, Center, Justified,** or **Bottom**.

5. In the **Apply To** box, indicate what section of the document you want these changes to affect (apply).

6. If you are creating a template and you want these changes to be in effect with all new documents using the same template, click **Default**, and then click **Yes**.

7. Click **Ok**.

Indenting

Both Sides of Paragraph

Another way to add a touch of professionalism to your document is through the efficient use of indentations. The applications of indentations are for vari-ous reasons. At times, you can use it to draw the reader's attention to a specific area of a document. Margins are usually applicable to the entire document or sections within the document, but paragraph indentations apply to one or more paragraphs. To indent both sides of a paragraph, follow these steps:

1. Make sure the cursor (the insertion point) is blinking in the beginning of the paragraph you want to indent, or simply select multiple para-graphs to indent.

2. Choose **Format → Paragraph**, and when the following Paragraph dialog window is displayed; click the **Indents and Spacing** tab (if not already selected).

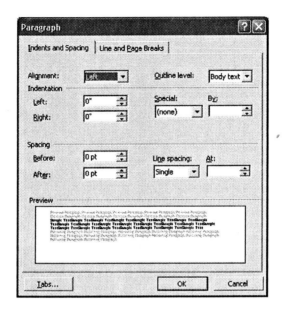

3. Under Indentation, type or select a value in the **Left** and do the same thing for the **Right** box.
4. Click **Ok** to apply the indentation to the paragraph(s) you selected.

First Line

There are some people who prefer to have the first line of every paragraph of their modified block style for letters or documents indented. Regardless of the style you prefer you can use the **Format → Paragraph** command to indent the first line of every paragraph of your letter or document.

Steps

Make sure the cursor (the insertion point) is blinking in the beginning of the paragraph you want to indent, or simply select multiple paragraphs to indent.

1. Choose **Format → Paragraph**.
2. Click the **Indents and Spacing** tab.
3. Click the box under **Special** to select **First Line**.
4. In the **By** box, type a new value or accept the 0.5" default indentation setting.
5. Click **Ok**.

Other possible indentations

Increase and Decrease Indent

You can use the Increase Indent and Decrease Indent buttons on the **Formatting** toolbar to move a paragraph inward (increase) or outward (decrease). The **Formatting** toolbar buttons by default is set at 0.5." If you have not changed Word's default tabs, you will discover that they are still set at 0.5" across the line.

Steps

1. Move the cursor to either the beginning or the end of the paragraph to be indented, or select multiple paragraphs to indent.
2. Click the **Increase Indent** button to indent the paragraph(s) 0.5" per click.
3. Click the **Decrease Indent** button to decrease the indent 0.5" per click.

Hanging Indent

When it comes to dealing with bulleted or numbered lists, glossary items, and bibliography entries, hanging indent is more appropriate. The first line of the paragraph doesn't move, while the remaining lines of the paragraph move to the right at the indent location.

Steps

1. Make sure the cursor (the insertion point) is blinking in the beginning of the paragraph you want to indent, or simply select multiple paragraphs to indent.
2. Choose F**o**rmat → **P**aragraph.
3. Click the **I**ndents and Spacing tab.
4. Click the box under **S**pecial to select **Hanging**.
5. In the **By** box, type a new value or accept the 0.5" default indentation setting.
6. Click **Ok**.

Adding Drop Cap

I n case you are wondering what is a drop cap? A *drop cap* is a large capital letter usually of the first word of the first line of a paragraph. This large capital letter aligns with the top of the first line of the paragraph but successive line or lines (depending on the size of the capital letter) are indented for adequate space. "Drop caps usually mark the beginning of key sections or major topics in a document."

Steps

1. **Highlight the first letter** of the first word of the paragraph you want to change into a drop cap.

2. Choose **Format → Drop Cap** to display the Drop Cap dialog window.

3. Under **Position**, select **Dropped**.

4. In the **Options** section, select the **Font** from the drop-down list (select Times New Roman, or any font of your choice)

5. Change the **Lines to Drop** from the default three (3) to two (2)

6. To change the distance of the text from the drop cap, use the increment buttons on the **Distance from Text** option

7. Click **Ok**.

Notepad

To remove drop caps, simply click the drop caps text, choose Format → Drop Cap, click the None option in the Position section of the dialog window, and then click Ok.

Useful Shortcuts on Indentation

Action	Shortcut
Move the left indent to the next tab stop—inward.	Ctrl + M
Move the left indent back to the preceding tab stop—outward	Ctrl + Shift + M
Create a hanging indent	Ctrl + T
Undo the hanging indent by moving back to the preceding tab	Ctrl + Shift + T
Remove indentation all together	Ctrl + Q

Alignment

By design, Word (like any other word processor) automatically aligns text to the left. Accepting this type of alignment depends on your type of document or preferences. The question then becomes "To be or not to be?" You have a choice. Some of the choices available to you include; changing the alignment to center, right, full justified, or back to left.

As you have seen in the letterhead we created earlier, the address of MidMed is aligned right. You can do the same thing for newsletters, brochures, agreement or formal business letters. The choice of which alignment is right for you is entirely up to you. Let us take a careful look at some alignment currently available in Microsoft Word.

Align Text Horizontally

To call the attention of your system to the area of your text you are going to align, you need to first select (highlight) the area. It could be a word, a phrase, paragraph or paragraphs.

On your **Formatting** toolbars, look for these buttons: They are arranged in the following order

1. Align Left
2. Center
3. Align Right
4. Justify

To align your text, follow these steps

1. Select (highlight) the text you want to align

2. To align left press **Ctrl + L** or simply click on the button that says **Align Left**

3. To centralize press **Ctrl + E**, or click on **Center**

4. To align right press **Ctrl + R**, or click on **Align Right**

5. To justify press **Ctrl + J**, or click on **Justify**.

Align Text Vertically

If you want to deviate from the way Microsoft Word aligns text to the top margin, there is no law against that (wow, isn't that good to know!). As far as Microsoft Word is concerned, your wish is his command. You may need to align your text a little differently, most especially if you are trying to create a report cover. To accomplish this goal, follow these simple steps

1. Move the cursor to the beginning of the text you want to align.

2. Choose **File** → **Page Setup** to display the Page Setup dialog window.

3. Click the **Layout** tab, and then click the box under **Vertical Alignment list,** and select **Center**, or **Justify**, or **Top**, or **Bottom** to change the alignment.

4. In **Apply To list** box, select whichever is appropriate, and then click **Ok**.

Inserting Newspaper style Columns

Another way to beautify your document is through the use of columns. By default, the standard Word layout is newspaper style, in which all columns are the same width, and text flows from the top of the first column down to the bottom of the column unto the top of the next and continue that way until every column is populated with text page after page just like you see in this section. (If I were you I would try this over and again).

Creating Columns of Equal Width

1. Click the **View** menu to switch to **Page Layout View** (in *Word 2000 and XP—2002*, the same is known as **Print Layout View**), or you can simply click Page Layout View or Print Layout View button displays at the bottom left corner of the document window before you get to the Taskbar, you should see these buttons:

2. You can choose to format an entire document with columns, or just a section of it.

3. On the Standard toolbar, click the **Columns** button .

4. Move the **mouse pointer** to select the number of columns. The same screen should indicate the number of columns selected. Select **2 columns** and click when your mouse is on the second column. Another way to do it is:

5. Choose **Format → Column** and that will activate the following screen:

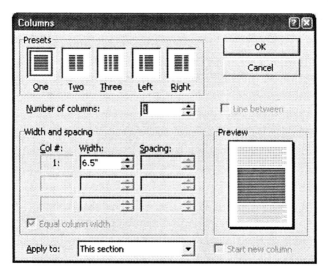

6. Click **Two** and adjust **Spacing** as you like. The default for spacing is usually 0.5"

Notepad

To insert columns in text frames, or comment boxes, and even headers and footers (if that becomes a choice for you), it is advisable to use a table. Newspaper columns are not currently available in headers and footers, comment boxes and frames of Microsoft Word.

Balancing Column Lengths

Steps

1. Click to be sure your cursor is blinking at the end of the text in the last column of the section you want to balance.

2. Choose **Insert → Break** to display the following Break dialog window:

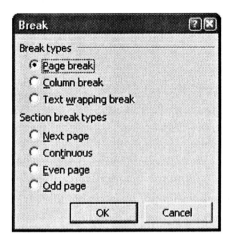

3. Click the radio button next to **Con̲tinuous** under **Section break types** and then click **Ok.**

Creating Columns of Unequal Width

Steps

1. Highlight (Select) **the text you want to format** into columns
2. Choose **Fo̲rmat** → **C̲olumns** to display the **Columns** dialog window as in the previous page.
3. Under **Presets,** click to select **L̲eft** or **R̲ight** option (depending on your preferences) to create two unequal columns.
4. In case you want more than two columns, feel free to increase the number in the **N̲umber of Columns** box.
5. If necessary, adjust the dimensions in the **Wi̲dth** and **S̲pacing** sections for each column, and then click **Ok.**

Remove, Increase, or Decrease Column(s)

Steps

1. Select **the text** of the column(s) you want to remove.
2. Choose **Format** → **Columns** and under **Presets** click **One** to remove columns
3. Under **Presets** click **Two** to increase. Or use the box next to **Number of Columns** to increase or decrease, or
4. Click **Columns** on the **Standard** toolbar and simply select one column to decrease.

Formatting

Find and Replace

The Find and Replace feature is one of the most important features of Microsoft Word. It enables you to search for and optionally replace a specific text or styles with another text or style. For example: Lets assume you would like to find the word "Clinician" and replace it with "Psychiatrist," All you need to do is follow the simple steps outlined below:

Steps

1. Choose **Edit** → **Replace** (or press **Ctrl + H**) to open the **Find and Replace** dialog window:

2. Click to place the cursor in the **Find What** text box, and type the word you want to find and replace.

3. Use the **Tab** key on your key board to move to the **Replace With** text box, and type the word you want to replace with.

4. Click the **Find Next** button to begin the search.

5. When the first occurrence is found, you can choose to **Replace** the first occurrence only or **Replace all**.

6. When you're finished, click the **Close** or **Cancel** button (depending on your version of Word) to close the **Find and Replace** dialog window.

Notepad

While in the Find and Replace dialog window, feel free to experiment with the More>> button to some of the options available such replacing special characters or defining what exactly to search and replace.

Paragraph Spacing

It is easier to customize the paragraph spacing in Microsoft Word for the exact spacing of your choice either between paragraphs or between the lines in a specified paragraph.

Steps

1. Mover the cursor anywhere in the paragraph to be modified, or high-light (select) the entire paragraph.

   Choose **Format** → **Paragraph** to display the following dialog window:

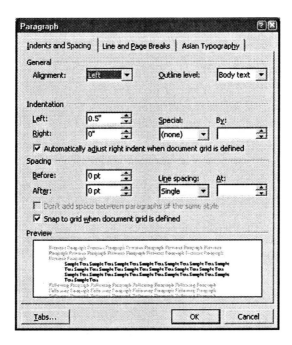

2. Click the **Indents and Spacing** tab if not already active.

3. Under **Spacing,** select **Before** and **After** to increase or decrease by points the number of lines before or after a paragraph (6 points = 1 line). However, my advice to you is to leave the **Before** and **After** at zero (0) unless you really have to change it, and then

4. Click the **drop-down arrow** under Line Spacing to choose from **Single** or **1.5 lines, Double,** or **At least,** or **Exactly,** or **Multiple.**

5. If you choose **At least,** or **Exactly** or **Multiple** options, you will have to enter a number in the **At** text box.

6. Click **Ok** when you finish.

Notepad

If you are not happy with the choices made, you can always use the **Undo** button or **Ctrl + Z** to return your document or paragraph to the way it was before changes were made.

Long Documents and Bookmarks

As you have read on page 36, working on a long document can sometimes require that you stop to do something else such as look for more information or simply take a break. Getting back to where you left off can be difficult to remember most especially if you are concerned as to where certain information appears in the document.

To minimize chances of having to go from page to page in search of where you saw whatever it is you are looking for; Microsoft Word makes it possible to navigate your way around easily without having to spend valuable time looking endlessly. One of the things you can do is to use hidden bookmarks. Using hidden bookmarks are very easy to do and you can easily put them anywhere depending on the information you are looking for.

Applying Bookmarks

1. Go to the exact location in your document where you want to place a bookmark and click.
2. Choose **Insert** → **Bookmark**. And when the following dialog window pops up

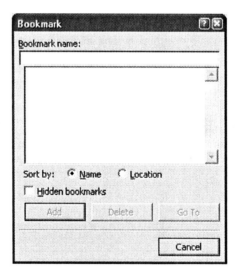

3. Type any name for your bookmark in the **Bookmark name,** and then
4. Click **Add.**

Using Bookmark to find a location

1. Press **F5** to open the **Find and Replace** dialog window.
2. Click the **Go To** tab.

3. You don't have to necessarily click **Bookmark** under **Go To What**. All you need to do is simply type the bookmark name in the field under **Enter page number**.

4. Click "**Go To**" to get to the information you bookmarked.

Add Watermarks to personalize your documents

Watermarks are good for indisputable authenticity. It is simply a text (usually a one word text or phrase) that appear behind the main text. You can also use picture, graphic or logo as watermark within your text. You can use it to identify the document's source or status of a document. Adding a watermark to a document is now easier than ever.

To add a watermark

1. Choose **Insert** → **Picture** → **WordArt** and when the following windows pops up

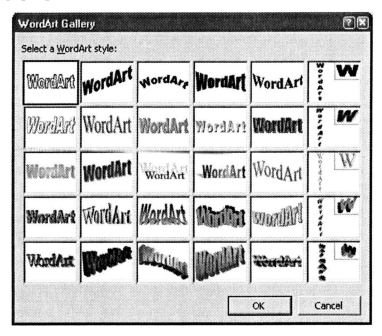

2. Click second column of the first row, and click **Ok**. That should lead you to the *Edit WordArt Text* screen.

3. Type the text you want to use as watermark, and click **Ok**.

4. If the text you just typed appears over your text don't panic. All you have to do is click on it (the WordArt text you just inserted).

5. Choose **Format → WordArt** and from the following window:

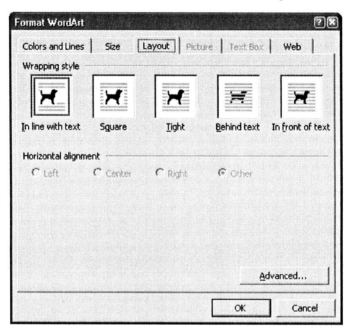

6. Click on the **Layout** tab and then click on the image in the **Behind text** box.

7. Click the **Colors and Lines** tab and under **Fill,** click in the field next to **Color** and on the color palette, select **Light Green.**

8. Under **Line,** click in the field next to **Color** and select **White.**

9. Click **Ok.** If the watermark is not well positioned, you can always click on it and drag to the location of choice to you.

Another way to insert watermark is to:

1. Choose **Format → Background,** and then click **Printed Watermark.**

2. "To insert a picture as a watermark, click **Picture watermark,** and then click **Select Picture.** Select the picture you want, and then click **Insert.**"

3. "To insert a text watermark, click **Text watermark,** and then select or enter the text you want."

4. "Select any additional options you want, and then click **Apply**."

5. "To view a watermark as it will appear on the printed page, click **Print Layout** on the **View** menu."

This last option may prove to be too difficult and almost impossible to see your watermark. To preview the watermark, click **View → Print Layout**, or, Click **File → Print Preview**, or wait until you print a hard copy of your document. However, I strongly recommend the first option.

Notepad

Headers and Footers

At times there is a need to create simple headers and footers with just company's name and address (letter head), or complex headers and footers that include company logo, document number, the name of the author, or any relevant information.

Formatting headers and footers are basically the same as formatting any part of your document. The only difference is that they are positioned at the top and bottom margins of each page with the default setting of 0.5"

Creating headers and footers

1. Choose **View → Header and Footer** to display the following **Header** pane (along with its floating toolbar)

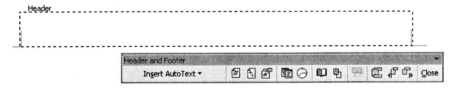

2. Type whatever information for your header, and to create a footer

3. Click the **Switch Between Header and Footer** which is the third button to the left of **Close** on the floating **Header and Footer** toolbar

4. To include **Page Number**, click the first button to the right of **Insert AutoText**. Next is the **Number of Pages**, followed by current **Date or Time**, and when you finish with the **Header and Footer** toolbar.

5. Click **Close** on the floating toolbar to return to your document.

Notepad

When you are creating header or footer, use the In**s**ert AutoText button on the **Header and Footer** floating toolbar to insert common entries such as the file name and page X of Y (total number of pages).

Inserting Page Numbers outside of Header and Footer

To make your long documents easier to read and reference, you need to insert page numbers. When you insert page number Word automatically formats them in the header or footer section of each document. You can then use the same techniques for working with headers and footers to format page numbers. Follow these steps to insert page numbers:

1. While in Normal view or Page Layout view (Print Layout View), choose **I**nsert → **Page N**u**mbers** to display the following dialog window.

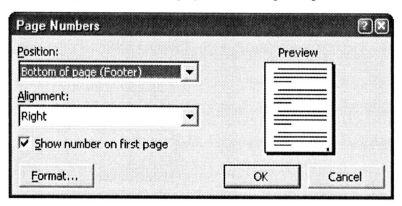

2. From the **P**osition list box, click to select one of the available two options: **Bottom of Page (Footer)**, or **Top of Page (Header)**.

3. From the **A**lignment list box, click to select where to place numbers on each page **Left**, or **Center**, or **Right**, or **Inside**, or **Outside**.

4. If you want to start page numbering from the first page, you've got to place a check mark in the box next to **S**how **Number on First Page**

5. There are still more selections you can make base on your preferences. Click the **F**ormat button and that should take you to the following **Page Number Format** dialog window.

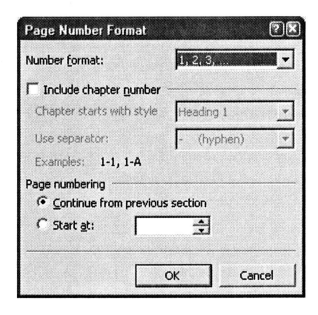

6. From this window, feel free to format page number as your document demand and after that,

7. Click **Ok** to return to the **Page Numbers** dialog window,

8. Click **Ok** or **Close** to return to the document page.

CHAPTER TEN

Document Layout and Printing

You may have noticed that this section seems to be the longest of them all. Bear with me just a little while longer. We only have a few more important topics to go over and I can't wait to finish. My little girl called and she's already looking forward to "Lizzie McGuire the Movie" with Hillary Duff. A little while ago it was "Like Mike" with Bow Wow. When are all these going to end? Anyway, let's hurry up and finish this section and the next one. Ok?

Creating Index

If you are creating a long document with so many pages and topics, you will find the use of **Index** very helpful. Index provides the page numbers where you can find whatever topic(s) you are looking for. "Without an index, readers will have difficulty locating information in long documents."

There are three steps to creating index. First of all, you must identify each entry you want to index. Next, you have to collect the marked entries into an index and the last step is to compile your index. Follow the steps outlined below to create index for your "Employee Handbook," "Business Description and Policy," and any other large document you are likely to deal with.

1. Highlight (select) the word or phrase you want to index (one word or one phrase at a time).

2. Choose **Insert, → Index and Tables** (if you are using Word XP, choose **Insert → Reference → Index and Tables**) to display the following dialog window.

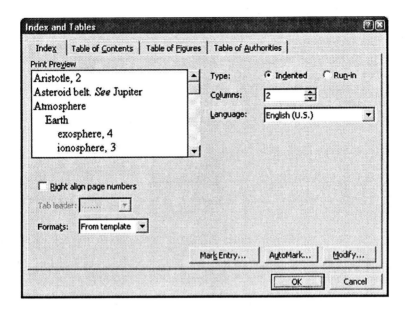

3. Click the **Index** tab (if not already displayed) to display available indexing options.

4. Choose the **Mark Entry** button to display the following **Mark Index Entry** dialog window.

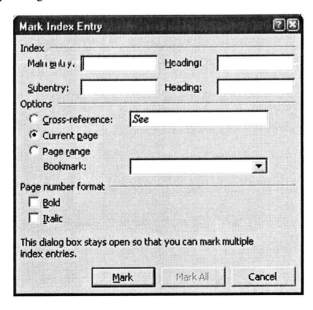

5. You should see the word or phrase you selected in Step 1 displayed in the **Main Entry** text box. To make changes to any of the texts, click in the text box to make your changes.

6. Under **Options,** click any of the radio buttons to select one of the index entry options—**Cross-Reference,** or **Current Page,** or **Page Range Bookmark,** and then choose the **Mark** button. Notice that the dialog window stays open so you can mark multiple entries.

7. Click outside of the dialog window (without closing it) to select the next word or phrase you want to mark, and when you finish, click on the dialog window and then repeat step 6 above. Again, the new word or phrase will be displayed in the **Main Entry** text box; choose **Mark** and repeat until all entries are marked.

8. When you finish marking all entries, click **Close.**

Compiling Index

The next action is to compile those entries into a list, usually in the back (the last page) of the document you just indexed. Follow these steps to compile your document:

1. Go to the location where you would like the index to appear and click to place the cursor at the beginning of that location. If any non-printing character including field codes is displayed, turn it off.

2. Choose **Insert → Index and Tables** to display the dialog window.

3. Choose the **Index** tab if it is not already active.

4. Click to select either of the radio buttons next to **Indented** or **Run-In** to indicate the type of index you want to build (as you select, watch the **Print Preview** section reacting to whichever button you click).

5. In the **Formats** list box, select from one of the several choices available, and watch the **Print Preview** area as it displays an example of what the index will look like base on your choice.

6. If you want the index in more than two columns, change the number in the **Columns** spin box.

7. In the **Tab Leader** drop-down list box, click to select the leader *style* you want to use.

8. Click **Ok** to compile the index.

Creating Forms

Forms are a valuable tool in any office environment. It is one of many ways to get people to interact thereby lighting the load of Administrative staff. Forms (soft forms such as Web forms or hard copy such as printed forms) are used to collect information. However, until a few years ago, creating forms (most especially web forms) was almost impossible for an average person. There was a time you think you needed a programming degree just to create forms. Thanks to advancement in technology, you can now do it without having to make anybody miserable.

Whether you are designing a soft form (for use in a Web page) or a hard copy form (printed form), elements required to design a form are basically the same. "Typically, forms you created are saved as templates so they can be used repeatedly. When filled out and saved, the template remains as you originally created it. Forms can be part of a document or an independent document. They may be short or several pages long." To design a form, follow these steps:

1. Choose <u>V</u>iew → <u>T</u>oolbars → Forms and move the form toolbar to a convenient place in the toolbar area on your Word screen.

2. Choose <u>F</u>ile → <u>N</u>ew to start a new document or, if you are going to insert the form in an existing document, click to place your cursor in the particular area where you want to begin designing your form.

3. Type the label for the first form field and then go to the **Forms** toolbar to insert a **Text Form Field**, or **Check Box Form Field**, or **Drop-Down Form Field**. If you are creating a hard copy form, don't be afraid to use **Underscore** to indicate your form field.

4. Repeat Step 2 until you complete your form design. Move your mouse over each button in the **Forms** toolbar to see some of the options available such as **Form Field Shading**, thereby use them to accomplish a well designed form.

5. Save the form as a template or as a Word document either way, you will be able to print it out.

6. If you are creating a Web form, it may be necessary to protect the form with or without the use of a password, click the **Protect Form** button in the **Forms** toolbar.

7. To include a password, choose <u>T</u>ools → <u>P</u>rotect Document to open the following dialog window:

8. Click <u>F</u>orms and then enter a password. Click **Ok** and that should activate **Confirm Password** dialog window, re-enter the exact same password and click **Ok**.

"Word document forms comprises of labeled fields where those
using the form enter text, toggle a check box on or off, or select
from a drop-down list. On screen form fields can perform
automatic calculations. The document should be protected so
that only data entered in the fields can be changed, not the text of the
document." Log on to www.mednetservices.com for more information
of forms.

Dealing with Graphics

At times you need to insert business logo, pictures, clip art, drawings, and in
the case of Web pages you may need to include movies, sound and music. This
group of possibilities is known as Graphics. However, dealing with them in
Microsoft Word is relatively easy to do. In a way, Word graphics such as drawings, picture, and clipart or business logo remains float on the page and text
can be designed to flow around them or simply remain as a stand alone
object. Floating makes it possible to drag the graphic from one location to a
new place in the document. For an in-depth discussion of graphics, visit
www.mednetservices.com

Inserting Clip Art

Inserting *clip art* and picture provides an easy way to add visual appeal to a document. Locating any of the images included in *Microsoft Word* is relatively easy. However, *Word XP (2002)* is designed to rearrange clip arts and other images in your system a little differently. More about that at www.mednetservices.com To insert Clip Art, carefully follow these steps:

1. Click to place the cursor at the exact location in the document where you want the image to appear.

2. Choose Insert, → Picture, → Clip Art to open the *Word 2000* Clip Art Gallery dialog window:

3. Click on the Clip Art tab to activate it (if not already activated).

4. Scroll through the categories and when you find a category of interest to you, click on the category and choose from the available Images in that category.

As you will discover, nearly all the different versions of Word currently available handles the issue of **Inserting Clip Art** differently. With Word 2000, you have the option to create new category and then import picture into the new category. However, in Word XP, you can have the program **Collect** every available **Clip Arts** in your system automatically. For more information, visit www.mednetservices.com

Wrapping Text

You can wrap text around almost any object—clip arts, business logo, picture, charts and even boxes. This is also known as controlling text flow. Take a careful look at the following real Newspaper Ad and you will see how the text flows around the object (a book entitled "Shrouded in Mystery"). To control text flow around any image, follow the steps outlined below:

Shrouded in Mystery:

A Look at the Deeds of Agent of Destruction— written by Nyher Gubloan.

This book reveals a senseless act of man's inhumanity to man that could have been avoided but those of evil intent went forth anyhow. This is a true story and it took place in Rhode Island—the smallest state in the union.

The book is now available at some local bookstores including Barnes & Noble Bookseller. You can also get a copy through any of the following websites: www.bn.com or www.1stbooks.com or www.amazon.com.

Steps (Word 2000 and Word XP—2002)

1. Click on the image to be sure you have the focus of the system on the image itself.

2. Choose F<u>o</u>rmat → **Picture**. When the **Format Picture** window pops up

3. Click the **Layout** tab, and then click any of the available images which indicate how the system will wrap text around the object. Available choices are: **In line with text** or **Square** or **Tight** or **Behind text** or **In front of text**.

4. You can also choose how to position the object within your text. Under **Horizontal Alignment** feel free to choose between; **Left** or **Center** or **Right** or **Other**.

Word Count

When it comes to document handling, setting limitation is not uncommon nowadays. Your project director may ask you to produce 2500 words or less. Perhaps you are responding to a Web request asking you not to exceed 500 words. Hey, lets face it, its not like you don't know how to count but when you know that the phone is going to ring in a few seconds or somebody is going to interrupt your concentration very shortly, why would you want to take on such a head spinning task anyway! If you are really looking for challenges, you are better off running with the bulls in Spain. But as far as word count is concerned, let your Microsoft Word do the counting for you. But don't blame me if you go over the requirement of your project and every idea look so great you don't know which one to delete. To keep track, follow this steps:

1. From Word 2000, click **File → Properties** and you should see the following pop up Window:

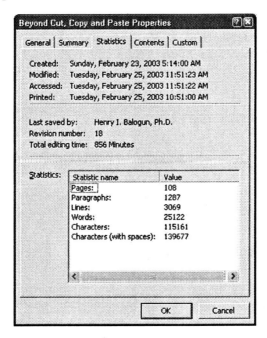

2. Click the **Statistics** tab and the **Statistics** window should display among other things, the number of words you have so far.
3. Click **Ok.**

4. From *Word XP—2002*, choose **Tools → Word Count** to count and recount as required

5. To use the new **Word Count** toolbar available only in Word XP, on the **View** menu, point to **Toolbars** and click **Word Count**. This should display the **Word Count** Toolbar at the bottom right corner in the toolbar area of your screen.

6. Then click **Recount** to update the count any time you want. You can also choose to see the current number of **characters, lines, pages,** and **paragraphs.**

Printing

Needless to say, we've covered a lot of interesting and useful topics and there is no better time to produce an excellent hard copy.

After you have previewed your document, you can send the document directly to a printer, thereby print the current page, a group of pages (page range), or the whole document. You can even compress a document to print two or more pages on one sheet of paper to avoid wasting papers during preview and proofreading.

Your document is not the only thing you can print in Microsoft Office. You can print pictures or any image. If you have created AutoText entries, like we did earlier, you may find it useful to print the list for reference. Not only that, If you have inserted comments in your document (like the feedback we received from the Clinical Director) to provide a note to yourself or other readers (in case you are a team member working on one large document), you may also find it useful to print those comments. I'm going to guide you as to how to print any of the following:

AutoText Entries, Comments and Key Assignments

Steps

1. You can print AutoText entries from any document window. Go to **File → Print** to display the following Print dialog window.

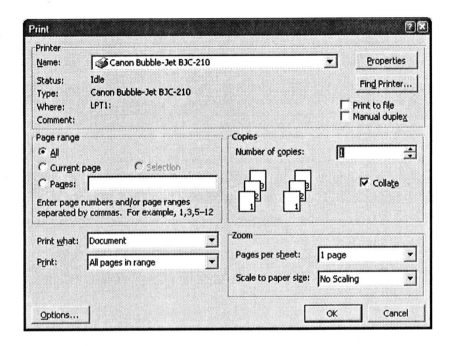

2. Click the option box next to **Print** **W**hat, and select **AutoText entries**.

3. Click **Ok** and you should see your *AutoText entry* prints with the abbreviation in bold on one line and the *AutoText entry* on another line.

4. To print **Comments** or **Key Assignments**, repeat step 3 but instead of AutoText entries, select **Comments** or **Key Assignments** and after that

5. Click **Ok**.

Documents Printing

If you are quickly going to print the entire document to the default printer, you may find that the **Print** button on the **Standard** toolbar is a lot faster to use. Word would not display the Print dialog window. However, if you are concerned about changing print options, the Print dialog window is no doubt, your best bet.

Steps

1. Choose <u>F</u>ile → <u>P</u>rint to display the Print dialog window shown on the previous page.

2. Click the drop down option box next to the <u>N</u>ame list box, and select the drop-down arrow.

3. Choose a printer. If you are on a network and have shared network printers installed, you will see it listed.

4. Click the **Properties** button to display available options for the currently selected printer.

5. Make appropriate changes with regard to **Paper, Graphics, Fonts,** and **Device Options** tabs—both the tabs and options may differ depending on the printer type.

6. Click **Ok** to return to the **Print** dialog window.

7. To print one copy of the whole document, leave the other options as they are and choose **Ok**.

8. To print more than one copy, feel free to adjust the **Number of Copies**

9. To **Collate**, click to put a check mark in the option box next to **Collate**. This will print one set of the same document at a time.

10. To print page range, under **Page Range** select **All** to print the entire document, or **Curr<u>e</u>nt Page** to print the page where cursor is located or blinking, or select **Pages** and type the page ranges you want to print. In Word you are not limited in how you can define your page range. For example: you can choose to print pages **22—28** (avoid using the word "to." To print pages 1, 8, and 18, you would type **1,8,18** (no space). Also, Word allows you to even mix range definitions; such as **1,8,18,22-28**.

11. Once you finish making changes, click **Ok** to start printing.

Printing two pages of text on one sheet of paper

We have to proofread what we have done so far to make corrections if we have to. But one thing we cannot afford right now is to waste papers and ink. Don't forget that part of the overall goal of this clinic is to minimize cost and maximize profit. We don't want our effort to result in wasteful spending. Fortunately for us, Microsoft Word 2000 and XP have a variety of ways to achieve this objective.

You can save paper by printing your document on both sides of the paper even if your printer does not support printing on both sides. Regardless, I'm going to show you how to do this without going over your budget.

1. Choose **File → Print**.

2. From the **Print** window under **Zoom** you can select two or more pages of a document to print on a single sheet of paper. One quick note: any action taken here will not change or affect the formatting and page layout of your document.

3. Click **Ok**.

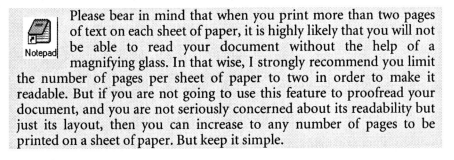

Please bear in mind that when you print more than two pages of text on each sheet of paper, it is highly likely that you will not be able to read your document without the help of a magnifying glass. In that wise, I strongly recommend you limit the number of pages per sheet of paper to two in order to make it readable. But if you are not going to use this feature to proofread your document, and you are not seriously concerned about its readability but just its layout, then you can increase to any number of pages to be printed on a sheet of paper. But keep it simple.

CHAPTER ELEVEN

Integration within Microsoft Office

Inability of one program to perform what other programs can do so very well is not really of a serious concern in Microsoft Office. You are well aware that there are some calculations you can perform in Microsoft Word table but on the other hand, there are a lot you wouldn't be able to do. However, if you are having problems doing those calculations in Word, you can simply walk across the isle (not literally) and bring Excel into Word and this is known as embedding. When you embed Excel worksheet into Word, you are in a way asking Excel to come into the Word suite with all its worksheets, formulas, menus and toolbars.

In this section, we are going to deal extensively with embedding Excel worksheets in Word Documents. This will lead us to do some of the complex calculations we would love to do in Word but could not do due to its limitations. The **Insert Microsoft Excel Worksheet** button on the **Standard** toolbar lets you embed Excel worksheet in Word document.

We've just been asked to send a memo to every Psychiatrist and Therapist including Case Managers to let them know that the Central Office is in the process of closing some cases. The closing is scheduled to affect patients who have not been back in the clinic within the last 60 days for whatever reasons. But before this closing, we have to inform each Psychiatrist, Therapist and Case Manager just in case they would like to contact any of those patients to inform them about the pending action of the central office.

Dealing with Memorandum

Regardless of which style you prefer, all memorandum styles contain, basically, the same elements. The lead words area is usually in double space and with the following elements:

```
To:
From:
Date:
Subject:
```

 The body of the memo comes next and is usually in single space. The last part of the memo could be a Reference, or an Attachment. To fully understand this, let us reproduce the following memo:

MidMed©

To: Psychiatrists and Therapists
From: Clinical Director
Date: March 24, 2003
Subject: Administrative Discharge

Our record indicates that the following patients have been in inactive status for more than 60 days and we are about to initiate administrative discharge. I'm hereby asking you to carefully review the following list and kindly contact those that are your patients to inform them of the pending action.

cc: Vice President of Operations

Embedding Excel Worksheets in Word

1. Click to place the cursor at the location where you want to insert Excel Worksheet. In our case, we are going to insert the worksheet after the last line of the only paragraph in the Memo. At the end of "inform them of the pending action," press **Enter.**

2. Click **Insert Microsoft Excel Worksheet** button on the **Standard** toolbar.

3. Move your mouse to cover all the rows and columns and click the mouse. Expand the worksheet to accommodate five rows and six columns

4. Enter the following information:

a. First row, **Column one** = Patient ID, **Column two** = First Name, **Column three** = Last Name, **Column four** = SS Number, **Column five** = Admission Date and **Column six** = Phone Number. Feel free to format the heading as you like.

b. In column one of the second row, type the following formula (no space anywhere):
=Left(B2)&Left(C2)&Right(D2,4) and press **Enter**

5. Choose **Data → Form,** and

a. Enter the following information (without comma) beginning from the first active field: First Name = **Avon,** Last Name = **Lady,** SS Number = **021-34-9191,** Admission Date = **12/25/2002,** and Phone Number = **215-555-1212**

b. Click **New** and enter the following two patients information (don't forget to click **New** again to enter the next information):

First Name: Sugar	Flowing
Last Name: Daddy	Alien
SS Number: 321-45-9494	645-34-9595
Admission Date: 01/21/2003	01/24/2003
Phone Number: 717-555-1212	610-555-1212

c.Click **outside** of the Excel Worksheet to return to the Word mode. When you have finished, your memo should look like this:

MidMed©

To: Psychiatrists and Therapists
From: Clinical Director
Date: March 24, 2003
Subject: Administrative Discharge

Our record indicates that the following patients have been in inactive status for more than 60 days and we are about to initiate administrative discharge. I'm hereby asking you to carefully review the following list and kindly contact those that are your patients to inform them of the pending action.

cc: Vice President of Operations

Copy an Excel Table in Word

Another way to handle the task we just finished is to complete the worksheet in Excel and copy it into Word document. The feature for this also provides the option to have Excel retain its formatting, and also match the table style in Excel with the copy in Word document. Not only that, changes made to the original will also reflect in the copy. Unfortunately, this feature is only available in Excel XP (2002). Follow the steps outlined below to copy a table from Excel to Word:

1. Open Excel, and select the table you want to copy.
2. On the **Edit** menu, click **Copy**, or right-click on the selected table and on the pop up menu, click **Copy**
3. Open **Microsoft Word** without closing Excel, and then click where you want to insert the table.
4. Click **Edit** and then click **Paste Options.**
5. To link the table so that it automatically updates when changes are made in the source (the original Excel copy), select **Keep Source Formatting and Link to Excel,** and otherwise select **Keep Source Formatting.**

Insert PowerPoint Presentation in Word

You can include a PowerPoint presentation in a Word document. It also provides the option to have PowerPoint retain its formatting, and also match the presentation style in PowerPoint with the copy in Word document. Again, changes made to the original will also reflect in the copy. This is a PowerPoint XP (2002) feature and not available in Word 2000. Follow the steps outlined below to copy a presentation from PowerPoint to Word:

1. Click the area in your Word document where you want the PowerPoint presentation to appear.
2. Choose **Insert** → **Object** to open the following **Object** dialog window.

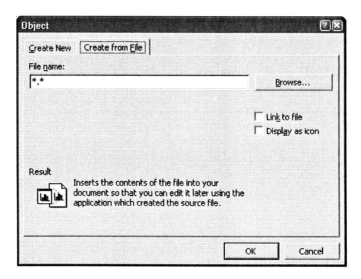

3. Click to activate **Create from File** tab.

4. To link the original presentation in PowerPoint to a Word document, click the check box next to **Link to File**.

5. Click **Browse** to locate the presentation file, and the system should immediately bring you to **Browse** window.

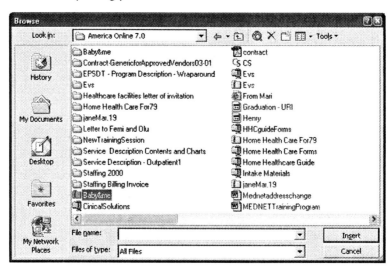

6. Locate and click the appropriate PowerPoint presentation file and click **Insert**.

7. You will see the first of the presentation showing in your Word document.

8. To play the presentation, **double-click** the slide in the Word document, sit back and enjoy.

More on this and some other incredible program features available in Microsoft Excel, and PowerPoint coming up in volume two. Register at www.mednetservices.com to reserve your copy of this amazing series

CHAPTER TWELVE

The Next Step

Maria: Hey doc! Thanks for helping us out. I really appreciate it.

HB: Anytime Maria! I really enjoyed every minute with you guys

Maria: By the way, there is a request from the Vice President of Operations. He is Ms. Jones' boss.

HB: What is the request?

Maria: Oh, he just wants to know if you can teach him Web Development and Internet programming in one week as soon as you finish helping us on the Excel and PowerPoint part of the current training.

HB: One week? Does he really understand what goes into Web Development and Programming? You know, stuff like HTML, DHTML, Flash, E-Commerce, Java Script, ASP, Visual Basic Script, Protocol, using proper syntax, nesting and server side programming! Do you know that those protocols can really make your head spin? You know what I'm talking about? How is it possible, for anyone, to teach that in one week?

Maria: I don't know doc! The guy is really serious.

HB: Serious about what? C'mon, these are really mind bending stuff. Does he have another request?

Maria: Yeah! According to him if you can't teach him about the Web Development and Programming in one week, he would like to know... (He heard that you guys are really smart and intelligent). He would like to know if you can explain to him how to understand women!

HB: How to understand women? Are you kidding me!

Maria: No sir! That's exactly his request.

HB: Well, what can I say! Go and ask him how soon does he want to start the training?

Maria: What? The Web Development and Programming training?

HB: No the cooking training—of course the Web Development training. What's the matter with you? By the way, tell him that we cannot start until we finish the Excel and PowerPoint part of the present training. Tell him that the official name of the Web training is going to be "Beyond e-mail." I'll see you guys tomorrow.

Maria: Great! You are indeed a God-send. This is very kind of you doc.

HB: Ok Maria, go get my friends—Bill, Steve and Scott on the phone. I'm not going to do this by myself.

Maria: You mean Bill as in Bill Gates, Steve as in Steve Case and Scott as in Scott McNealy—the power brokers of the binary and digital world? Wow! This is incredible. Can I turn down the music? I'm beginning to like it around here.

HB: Do not touch my Reba, ok?

Maria: Hey doc, do you ever listen to anything else besides Oprah, Reba, Alicia Key, Trisha Yearwood, Deborah Cox, Ashanti and of course— Beyonce and J. Lo?

HB: What is this? A pop quiz? Or is my choice of television shows and music on trial here? Please tell me you are not a TV reporter pretending to be a Secretary!

Maria: No doc! I'm not.

HB: Great! Now, go and make the call and I'll see you guys tomorrow. Don't forget, to tell the VP that the name for his training is going to be "Beyond e-mail." But we have to finish part two of the current one before doing anything new, ok?

Maria: Ok doc. Goodnight!

ABOUT THE AUTHOR

An experienced psychotherapist, healthcare administrator and Instructor, Dr. Balogun works with diverse population in outpatient psychiatry and also in home health care. He has been at various times a teacher of computer applications at the Bucks County Community College in the Adult Literacy Dept, a Small Business Development (SBD) consultant for Bryant College, Community College of Rhode Island and Salve Regina University. He was the President and CEO of Hengrab Medical when he received the Distinguished Leadership Award for Outstanding Service to the Health Care Profession by the American Biographical Institute. He is currently the CEO of MedNet Healthcare Systems, a public speaker, writer and a consultant.

He is a much sought-after consultant in home health care as well as Outpatient Psychiatry—most especially in startup, management and the development of effective growth strategies. He has conducted a lot of training in Medical Billing and Practice Management in Massachusetts, Rhode Island, New York, Pennsylvania, and Georgia.

Beyond Cut, Copy and Paste is the beginning of a series. A series designed to educate you, thrill you and lift your spirit. The next step after volume two of this incredible project is **Beyond e-mail.**

INDEX

P

R

S

T

U

W

0-595-27339-4

Printed in the United States
23694LVS00004B/195